Table of Contents

DELVE INTO KEY FINANCIAL, STATISTICAL, AND TIME FUNCTIONS

USING SOLVER TO KNOW THE OPTIMAL PRODUCT MIX

SECURE YOUR WORKBOOK DATA AND DESIGN WITH A PASSWORD.

Excel Workbook - Mark as Final

IMPROVE BUSINESS ANALYSES BY ADDING INTELLIGENCE AND KNOWLEDGE TO YOUR MODELS

CALCULATE LOAN PAYMENTS, INTEREST COSTS, TERMS, AND AMORTIZATION SCHEDULES

INTRODUCTION

How to Budget in Excel: Step-by-Step Guide

Let us face it: even with several market-based budgeting apps and software programs, finding a program that allows your one of a kind needs can be testing. Additionally, while a few projects are free, others aren't, putting more on your pile of month to month tabs. In case you're attempting to set aside cash and utilize your time astutely, the exact opposite thing you need is to blow both on a confounded program that doesn't fit well.

Open Excel.

Making a budget spreadsheet in Excel may seem like a daunting task, especially if you don't regularly use it. Trust me; you don't should be an Excel spending structure bookkeeper. This bit by bit guide will show you how to cause a financial plan in Excel that to can be immediately tweaked to meet the planning needs of your family.

So what are you saying? Let's just continue!

How to budget with Premade Templates?

The simplest and time-conscious way to create an Excel budget template is using Excel's premade templates library. If you are not sure where to commence, I strongly suggest starting with one of the software's budget templates to get a sense of what you may want to include in your own budget.

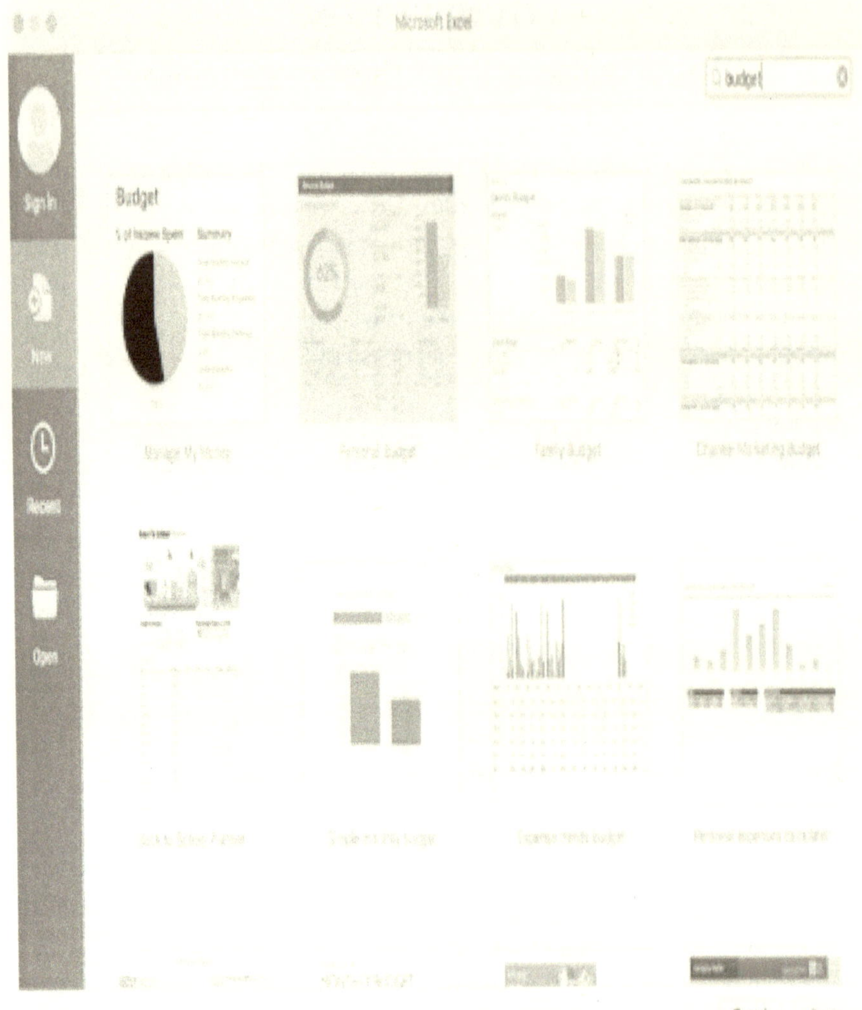

When opening Excel, simply go to File > New, then search for the term "budget." Several budget templates pop up, such as a family budget, personal expense calculator, holiday budget, and more.

For instance, if I went with the family budget spreadsheet, on the first tab, I'd get a premade spreadsheet with an income outline. In this window, you can change your family name and budget title, but don't mess with anything with a formula. Clicking on "7,200" will show "= Income[[#Totals],[Projected]]" next to the fx input box. Play the formulas and mess with the automated calculations that make Excel a breeze to use.

In the other two pages, you can find places to enter your data – monthly income and monthly cost. These figures automatically feed cash flow information to keep track of how much you earn and spend.

Customizing a template
To add to the already existing template, simply select where to add a box and right-click. Scroll down to "Insert" and choose either "Left Table Columns" or "Table Rows Above." This should automatically synchronize new information with existing tabs. If not, select the small down arrow next to the

"Projected" column, and you can include your new column in calculations.

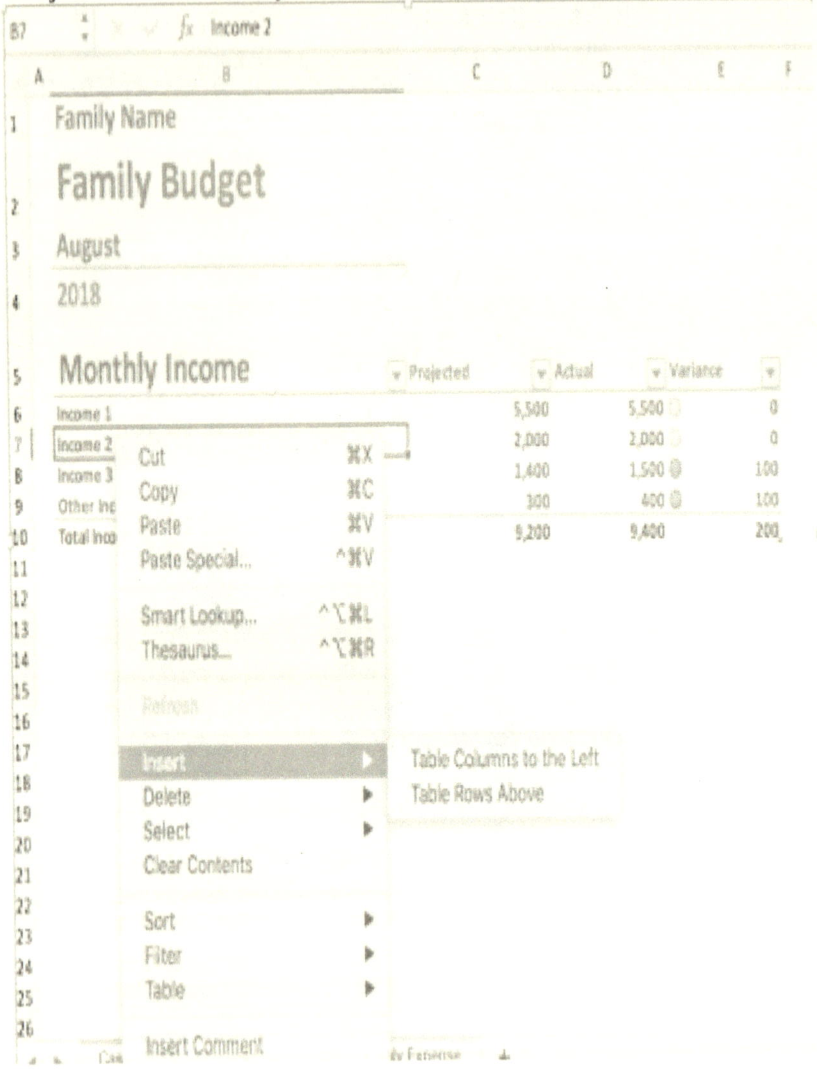

You may also remove unnecessary pieces. For example, if in your Monthly Expenses tab, you don't need the loans row, just right-click the tab, select "Delete" and "Table Rows."

It's as easy as that!

How to make a budget in Scratch

Need more budget customization? You could also create an Excel budget spreadsheet! Here's how to make a budget from scratch, including some of my favorite tips and tricks to customize your new budget.

Step 1: Blank Workbook

Your goal here is to build a zero-based budget for every dollar you spend and receive. It's a great way to track your money because it's so accurate. Honestly, once you start using this kind of budget, I don't think you'll ever use another budget style again.

Start by selecting the "Blank Workbook" or go to File > New > Blank Workbook. Now start with a fresh canvas.

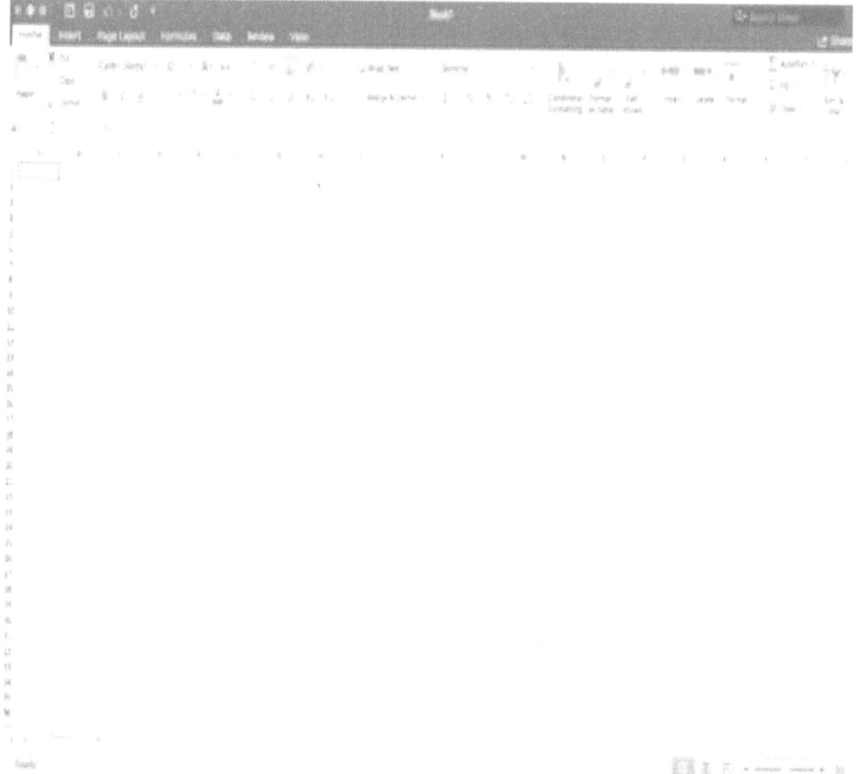

Stage 2: Set the profit tab

Once you have a blank workbook, block a chunk of columns as a month heading. Select the first 2 rows in columns A-G and pick "Merge and Center" from the "Back" section of the workbook. That'll make the whole section A1, and you can label it as you want.

Next, select A3-A11 cells, choose "Merge and Center," and write and center the word "Income." If you want creativity, choose different fonts and colors. Then combine B3 & C3 cells and mark them as "Source" to show where your income is generated, i.e., your main paycheck, side gig, etc. You'll want to merge each B&C row individually through row 11.

Mark cell D3 as "Date" to help track when this payment arrived. Adding a section for the date is optional and helpful if your sources of income vary monthly. This may not be beneficial if regular paychecks.

Next, title section E3 as "Planned" or "Budgeted." That's the amount of income you're planning to enter. Section F3 is your "Actual" column, representing the actual amount of money that hits the bank account – hopefully, more than you planned. Finally, a "Difference" column in cell G3 would automatically track your planned and actual income difference.

Phase 3: Automate Formulas

To visually appeal to your budget template, select the entire section. Use the borders tool on the "Home" tab of the workbook (looks like a square divided into four) and choose "All Borders." You can also shade a few areas to make it easier to read.

Once you like your spreadsheet look, it's time to add formulas that will automatically track everything for you. For the example below, I added the B11 cell "Complete." However, you can add it to the edge; however, many income streams you want to report.

After getting your "Total" tab, pick everything in the "Anticipated" column and use the "AutoSum" function to get your monthly total. Alternatively, select the last line in that column and enter the formula "= SUM(E4: E10)." You'll want to replace the designations E4 and E10 with the range of cells you want to add together. Repeat for your "Real" and "Difference" column.

To measure the difference between your "Expected" and "Real" income automatically, enter "=SUM(F4-E4)" after each row. Replace F4 and E4 with cells that match your "Actual" and "Planned" sections. Repeat for every income board.

	A	Source	Date	Planned	Actual	Difference
August						
3		Source	Date	Planned	Actual	Difference
4		Ralph's Main	5-Aug, 19-Au	$3,000	$3,100	$100
5		Gina's Main	10-Aug, 24-A	$4,000	$3,000	
6		Side business 1	15-Aug	$500	$500	$0
7	Income	Side business 2	20-Aug	$450	$550	$100
8						
9						
10						
11		Total		$7,950	$7,150	

Step 4: Add expenses

Once your income section is calculated, it's time to calculate your expenses.

You can carry this out on the same sheet or begin a brand new sheet. To leave expenses on the same sheet, build and customize a new area under the "Income" section. Then make use of the same column headings — Due Date, Planned, Actual, and Difference — as you did before.

Build the same formulas as before, with one big exception. In the column "Difference," instead of using the formula "= SUM(Actual Number-Planned Number)," you must turn it around. You have to use the formula "= SUM(Planned Number-Actual Number)" to measure how much you pay.

If you prefer to list your expenses on a separate sheet, just click "Sheet 1" on the + sign at the bottom. Rename each sheet by right-clicking and selecting "Rename."

You can customize categories to your liking when listing expenses. Make it as vague as you want. The key is easy tracking your regular spending. Some people may want to track their natural gas, trash, and electricity separately, while others may want to lump it together as "useful."

	Category	Due Date	Planned	Actual	Difference
	Total		$7,950	$7,150	-$800
	Category	Due Date	Planned	Actual	Difference
	Mortgage	1-Aug	$1,500	$1,500	$0
	Groceries		$450	$600	-$150
	Utilities		$300	$290	$10
	Loans		$700	$700	$0
	Childcare		$1,000	$1,000	$0
	Car Insurance		$250	$250	$0
	Health Insurance		$500	$500	$0
	Gas		$250	$350	-$100
	Car Payment	15-Aug	$500	$500	$0
Expenses					
	Total		$5,450	$5,690	

Phase 5: Add Parts

Now it's getting fun! Add as many sections as you want. I added "Funds" and "Savings" in the example. You may notice I removed the "Difference" column from these sections, as we're not concerned about over-saving. If you would love to see how much extra you've saved, feel free to add them in.

	Account	Planned	Actual	
	Total		$5,450	$5,690	($240)
	Account	Planned		Actual
Funds	Emergency Fund	$500		$300
	Home Maintenance	$100		$25
	Holidays	$50		$0
	Total	$650		$325
	Account	Planned		Actual
	Retirement	$1,000		$500
	College	$500		$500
Savings	Total	$1,500		$1,000

Step 6.0: Final balancing

Once you've generated all the sections you want to track, knowing your running balance is crucial. Thankfully, your calculator can be buried in your drawer and monitored automatically in Excel.

If you keep everything on one sheet, it's super easy. Simply create another section at the bottom. Then label one row "Total Spending" and the other "Final Balance." It's an easy way to compare your planned total to your actual total.

To calculate the total budget, enter the formula "=SUM(Planned Expenses Total, Planned Funds Total, Planned Savings Total)." To measure your projected balance, using the formula "=SUM(Total Planned Spending – Total Planned Income)." Do the same for actual spending and balance pages, but use actual numbers instead.

Know, to get an accurate total, you must do the total spent minus the total profits.

In my fictional instance below, the budget is $115. Because we've listed it in a spreadsheet, it's super easy to see where the family's over-spent and under-earned. And that's the point – to make tracking your money as easy as possible, so you know where each dollar is spent.

		Account	Planned	Actual	
31					
32					
33					
34					
35		Total		$5,700	$5,940	($240)
36		Account	Planned	Actual	
37		Emergency Fund	$500	$300	
38	Funds	Home Maintenance	$100	$25	
39		Holidays	$50	$0	
40					
41		Total	$650	$325	
42		Account	Planned	Actual	
43		Retirement	$1,000	$500	
44		College	$600	$500	
45					
46	Savings	Total	$1,600	$1,000	
47			Planned	Actual	
48		Total Spending	$7,950	$7,265	
49		Final Balance	$0	($115)	
50					

Phase 6.1: Adding Other Numbers

If you've created separate sheets for your spending, savings, and other funds, choose which sheet to put on. You can either add the aggregate to the principal sheet or make another sheet for all adjusts.

B2 fx =SUM(Expenses!E24,Funds!D6,Savings!D5)

	A	B	C	D	E	F	G
1		Planned			Actual		
2	Spending	$7,950			$7,265		
3	Final	$0			$115		
4							
5							
6							
7							
8							
9							
10							
11							

For the model above, I named my sheets at the end, including another complete sheet. The complete sheet will ascertain the all-out arranged spending and last parity, just as the all-out spending and last equalization.

Snap the cell you need the aggregate to show up and enter the equation "= SUM(SheetName!Cell, SheetName!Cell, SheetName!Cell)." This recipe would be "= SUM(Expenses!E24, Funds!D6, Savings!D5)."Repeat for your expected number and real sum.

To measure the difference between your income and total expenditure, pick the cell you want to view. Then enter "= SUM(SheetName!Cell-Spending Cell)" In the example, "= SUM(Income!F11-D2)" This cell displays a negative number if you spent more than you won.

Stage 7: Graph (optional)
Using a graph is optional, but you can better see how much you spend. To build a pie chart or bar graph displaying your spending, you must first create a percentage column.

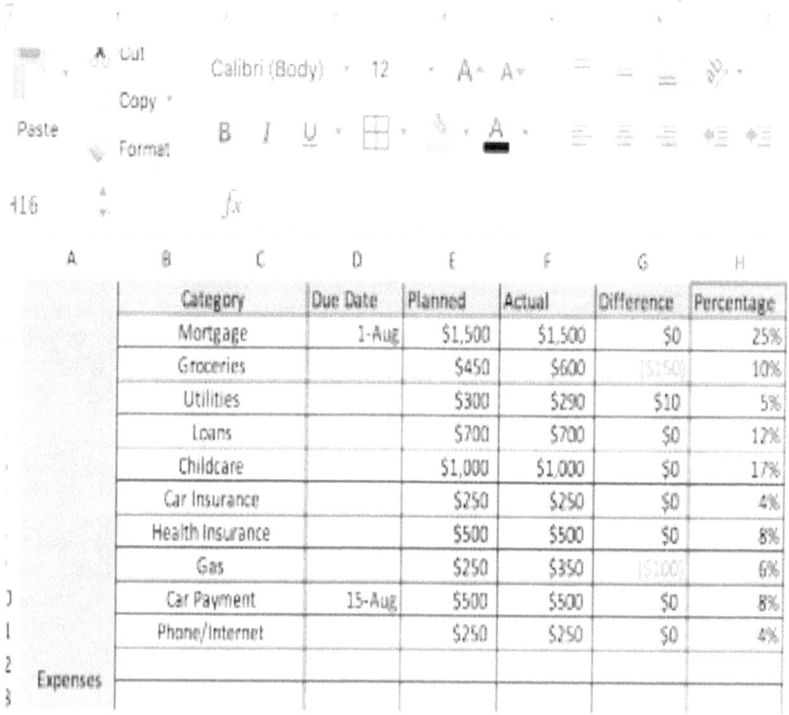

Category	Due Date	Planned	Actual	Difference	Percentage
Mortgage	1-Aug	$1,500	$1,500	$0	25%
Groceries		$450	$600	($150)	10%
Utilities		$300	$290	$10	5%
Loans		$700	$700	$0	12%
Childcare		$1,000	$1,000	$0	17%
Car Insurance		$250	$250	$0	4%
Health Insurance		$500	$500	$0	8%
Gas		$250	$350	($100)	6%
Car Payment	15-Aug	$500	$500	$0	8%
Phone/Internet		$250	$250	$0	4%

As the example shows, I just added another column. The formula is immediate "= Category Total Cell / Actual Total Cell." In our example, formula read "= F2 / F24."

Input this formula for every group as a percentage. To show the numbers as a percentage rather than a decimal, highlight the column and select "percent" to easily convert it to percentages. Your percentage should add up to 100%.

Category	Due Date	Planned	Actual	Difference	Percentage
Mortgage	1-Aug	$1,500	$1,500	$0	25%
Groceries		$450	$600	($150)	10%
Utilities		$300	$290	$10	5%
Loans		$700	$700	$0	12%
Childcare		$1,000	$1,000	$0	17%
Car Insurance		$250	$250	$0	4%
Health Insurance		$500	$500	$0	8%
Gas		$250	$350	($100)	6%
Car Payment	15-Aug	$500	$500	$0	8%
Phone/Internet		$250	$250	$0	4%

Simultaneously highlight the category column and percentage column. Once they are both highlighted, go to "Insert" and pick your graph type. If you don't like the style you've chosen, you can change it by right-clicking your graph and selecting "Change Chart Type."

The graph below is a donut map, and I like how it breaks down spending groups.

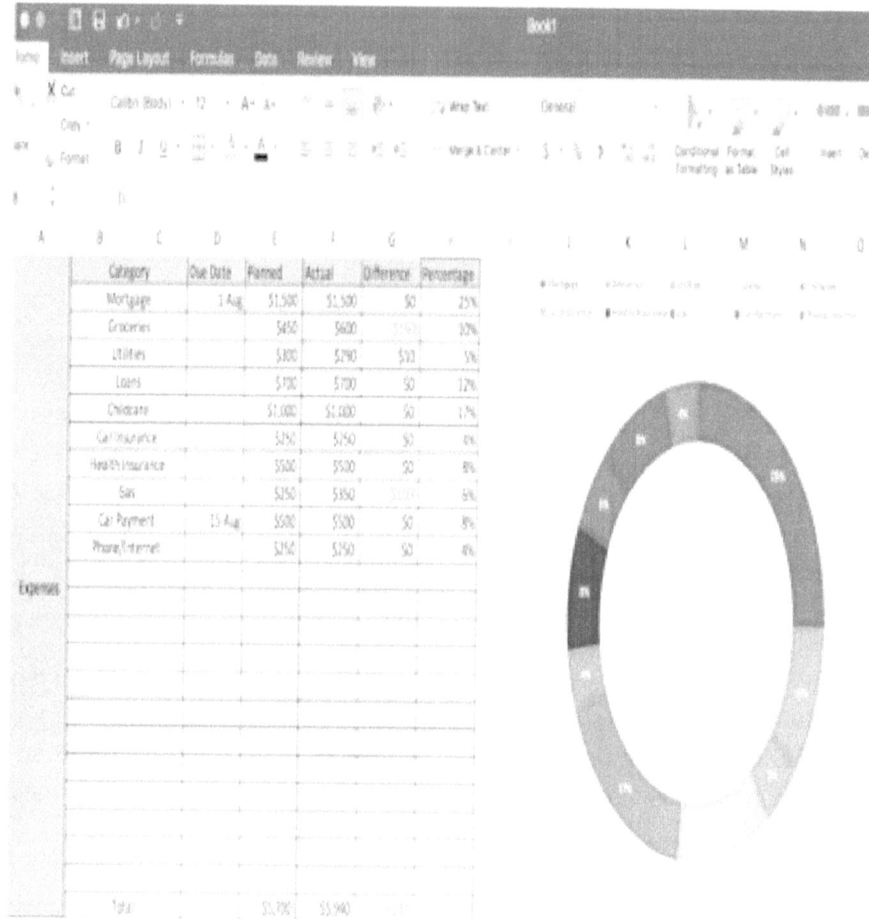

Creating a Budget Spreadsheet: Helpful

You could save your budget on Excel as a monthly template. If you kept one sheet of income, expenses, savings, etc., you can also copy all boxes and paste them on a new sheet. Rename that sheet for another month. This is a great way to spend all year in one Excel workbook. You can then create a new formula at year-end to add up your annual savings, spending, and earnings.

Excel will do the calculations automatically. I covered addition and subtraction, however here are multiplication and division formulas:

Multiplication: In the desired cell, type "=" accompanied by the cell for a number you want to multiply. Type "*" and end with the other number you want to multiply. Finally, enter hit. For example, "=F5*H50."

Division: type "=" in the desired cell, followed by the cell for a number to divide. Then type "/" and end with the other number you want to separate. Finally, enter hit. For example , " = E15 / A10.

Let's assume you want the bottom row to add all the numbers. Instead of typing the formula in each cell, you can speed up the process by dragging the same formula across a row. To do this, enter the recipe into one cell, click the cell after the all-out shows up, and drag the green box over the territory you need that equation to be applied. It's as straightforward as that.

Imagine a scenario in which You Don't Have Excel.

In the event that you love the idea of utilizing a spending spreadsheet; however, your machine doesn't accompany Excel, don't stress. Google offers a free form spreadsheet program called Sheets. The two frameworks look and capacity also. Also, Google Sheets works (nearly) consistently with Excel, which means you can without much of a stretch import an Excel spending format that you made into Sheets.

Make Succeed Your Own

While this guide explained how to make a budget in Excel, you're definitely not limited to what I've shown you. Excel is very customizable, and you could build a sheet to fit any financial area. Don't fear to create a whole new budget spreadsheet to track your holiday budget, holiday spending, debt repayment, and more.

Excel can be a key tool to transform your spending habits, so play around until you're comfortable. Once set up, automatic formulas in an Excel budget template can even trump budget pen and paper – at least in terms of convenience. Just enter the info correctly, and for you, everything will automatically populate. In addition, with a few clicks, you could easily view several months (or years) of data budgeting.

Here's the best part: if you don't want to, you never need to learn more than this guide. Sticking to a basic Excel budget template will work well for your money management, so don't feel like being an Excel genius. If you never know the other functions and options in Excel, but just follow these steps, you'll be perfect.

CREATING VBA AUTOMATE VARIOUS TASKS

For most of us, the road to Excel VBA programming begins with the need to perform some tasks with the standard tools in Excel. That task is different for us. Perhaps the job is to create separate workbooks for all rows in a data set. Maybe that task is automating emailing dozens of reports. Whatever the job is for you, you can bet somebody began their own trip to Excel VBA with the same need. The beautiful thing about Excel VBA is you don't have to be an expert to start solving problems. You may learn enough to solve a particular problem or go further and find ways to manage all sorts of automation scenarios. Whatever your goals will be, Excel 2019 Power Programming with VBA will help you leverage VBA's power to automate tasks, work smarter, and be more efficient.

What's VBA?

VBA's Visual Basic for Applications. Before moving into more depth, let's look at what computer programming is in a layman's language. Assume you've got a cleaner. If you want to clean the house and do the laundry, you tell her what to do, let's say English, and she does the job for you. As you work with a computer, you want to perform certain tasks. Just as you told the maid to do house chores, you can also tell the computer to do your tasks.

The process of telling the computer what to do is what is known as computer programming. Just like you used English to tell the maid what to do, you can use English to tell the machine what to do. English-like statements fall into high-level languages group. VBA is a high-level language you can use to bend Excel to your powerful will.

VBA is a subset of Visual Basic 6.0 BASIC stands for the All-Purpose Symbolic Instruction Code.

Why use VBA?

It uses English to write instructions.

Creating the user interface is like using paint. Just drag, drop, and align controls on the graphical user interface.

The quick curve of learning. From day one, you can start writing simple programs immediately.

Improves the functionality of Excel by making Excel behave the way you want it

VBA Personal & Business Applications

For personal use, use it for simple macros that automate most of your daily tasks. Read the Macros article on how you can do this.

For business, you can create powerful programs powered by excel and VBA. The pro of this approach is you can leverage excel's powerful features in your custom programs.

Visual Basic for VBA Applications

Before we can write some code, we must first learn the basics. The following basics help you get started.

Variable — we learned about algebra in high school. Find $(x+2y)$ where $x=1$, $y=3$. In this phrase, x and y are variables. Any numbers, i.e., 1 and 3, can be allocated as in this instance. They could also be switched to say 4 and 2. Variables are memory locations. As you work with VBA, you will need to declare variables as in algebra classes

Variables creation rules

O Don't use reserved words; if you're a student, you can't use the title lecturer or principal. These titles are reserved for teachers and school authorities. Reserved words are words with special meaning in Vba, and you can not use them as variable names.

O Variable names can't contain spaces – you can't define the first number. FirstNumber or first number.

O Use descriptive names – it's very tempting to call a variable, but prevent this. Use descriptive names, i.e., quantity, price, subtotal, etc. to make your VBA code readable.

Arithmetic operators-Brackets of Division Multiplication Addition and Subtraction (BODMAS) rules apply, so remember to apply them when using expressions that use multiple arithmetic operators. Like Excel, you can use

O+ Additional

O- Subtraction

O * Multiplication

O / O Division.

Logical operators- The definition of logical operators covered in earlier tutorials also applies to VBA research. This includes

O If comments are made

OR

NOT

AND

TRUE

FALSE

Activate Developer Option

Creating a new workbook

Select Start Ribbon button

Choose choices

Click Custom Ribbon

Select the developer checkbox as shown below

Click Okay

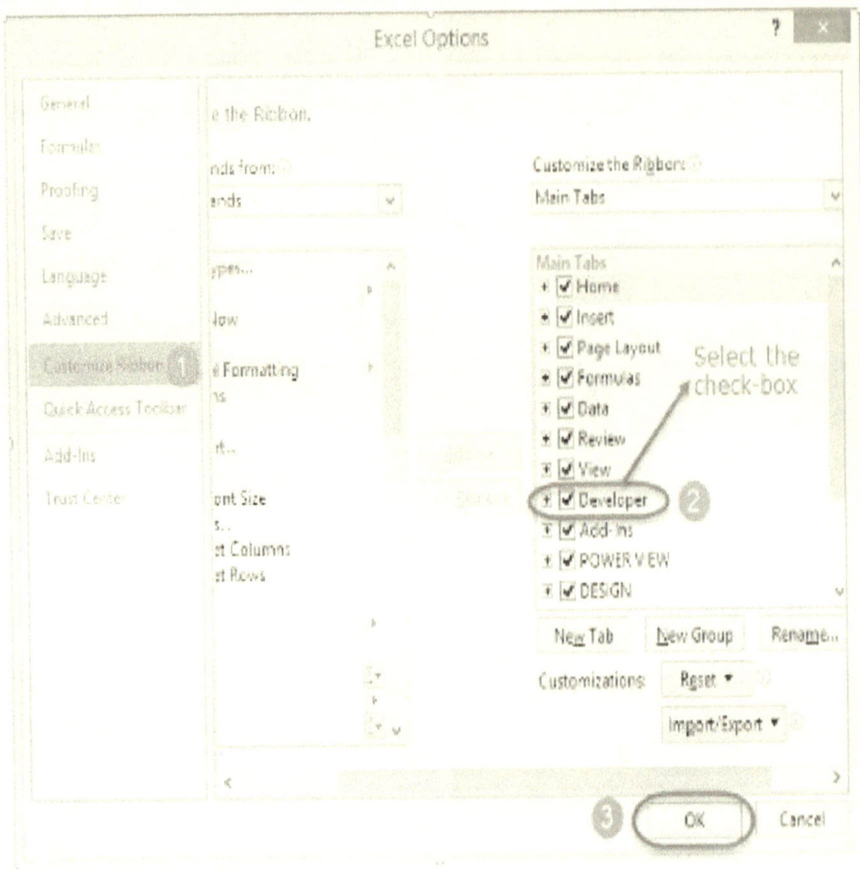

You can see the DEVELOPER tab in the ribbon

Hello world VBA

Now we'll show how to program in VBA. All programs must start with "Sub" and end with "End sub." Here's the name you want to add to your application. Although sub is a subroutine that we'll know later in the tutorial.
Undername

.

.

.

End of Sub

We'll create a basic VBA program that displays an input box to request the user's name and display a greeting message.

This tutorial assumes you've completed Macros in Excel tutorial and enabled DEVELOPER in Excel.

Creating a new workbook

Save in macro-enabled worksheet format * .xlsm

Click DEVELOPER tab

Click the INSERT button below the ribbon bar

Select a command button as shown below

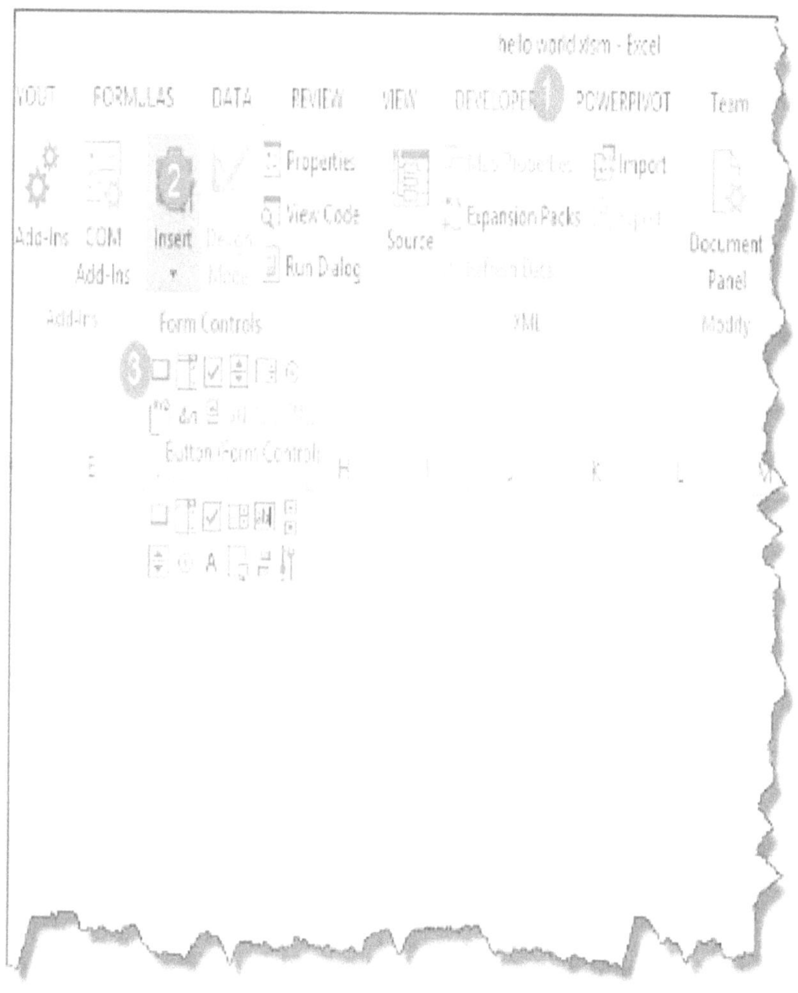

Draw the command button on the worksheet
You'll get the following dialog window

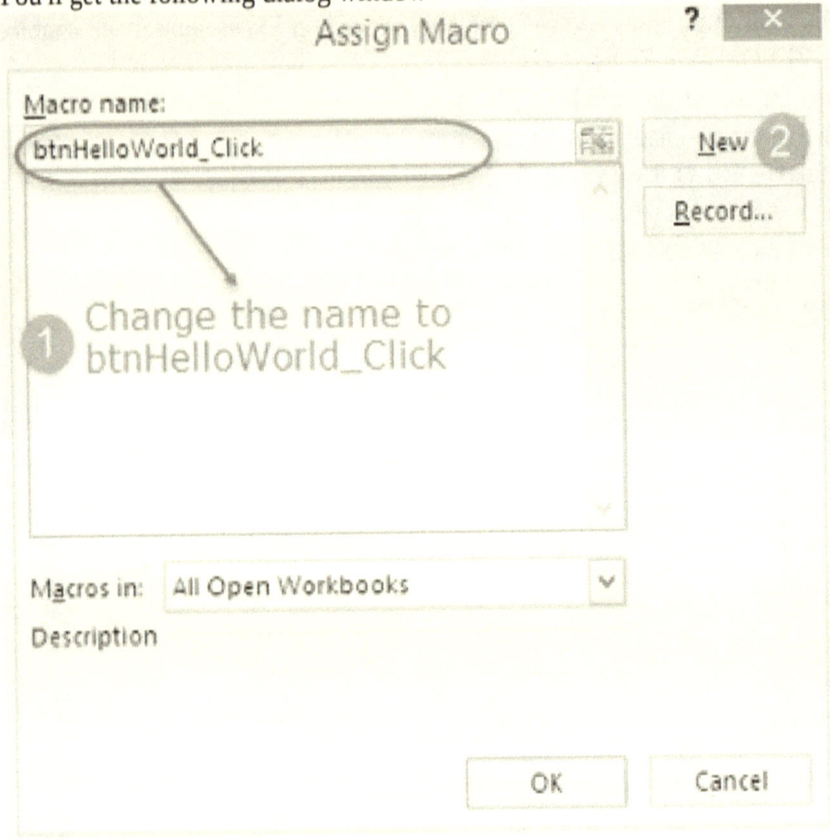

Rename macro to btnHelloWorld Click
Click New Button
You get the following code window

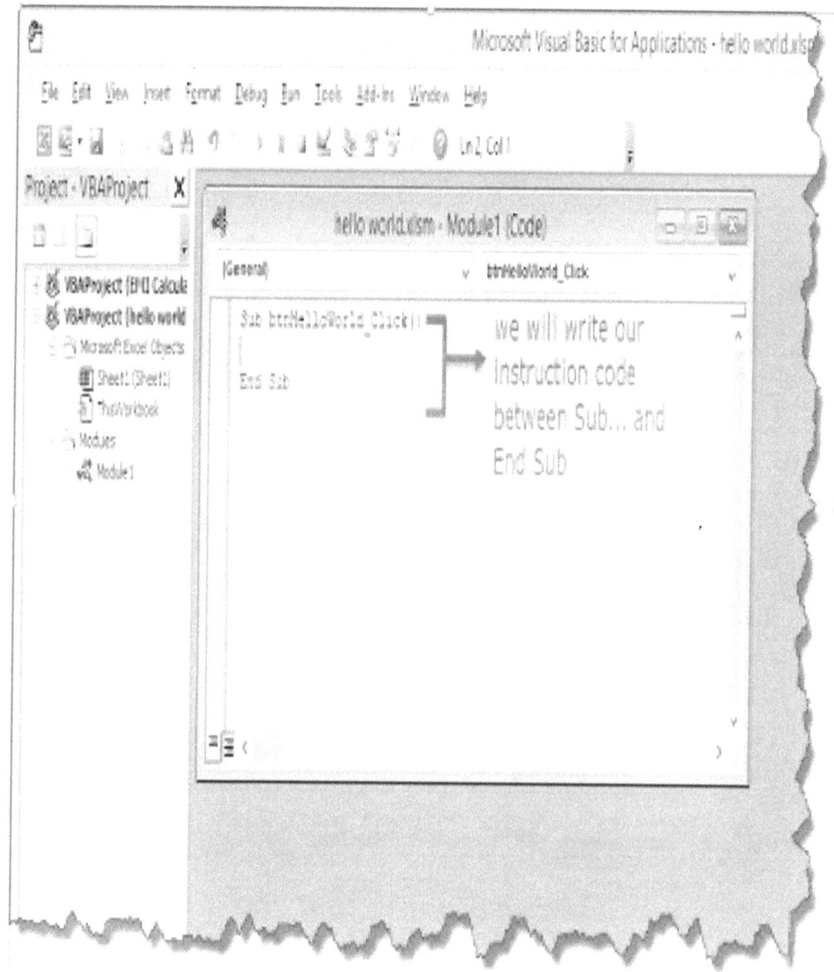

Enter the following instructions

Name As String

Name = InputBox("Enter name)

MsgBox "Hi"+name

HERE, HERE

"Dim name as string" generates a name variable. The variable accepts text, numeric and other characters, as we defined it as a string

"Name = InputBox("Enter Your Name") "calls the built-in InputBox function that displays a captioned window. The name entered is stored in the name variable.

"MsgBox" Hello "+name" calls the MsgBox function built to display, Hello, and the name entered.

Your full application window will look as follows.

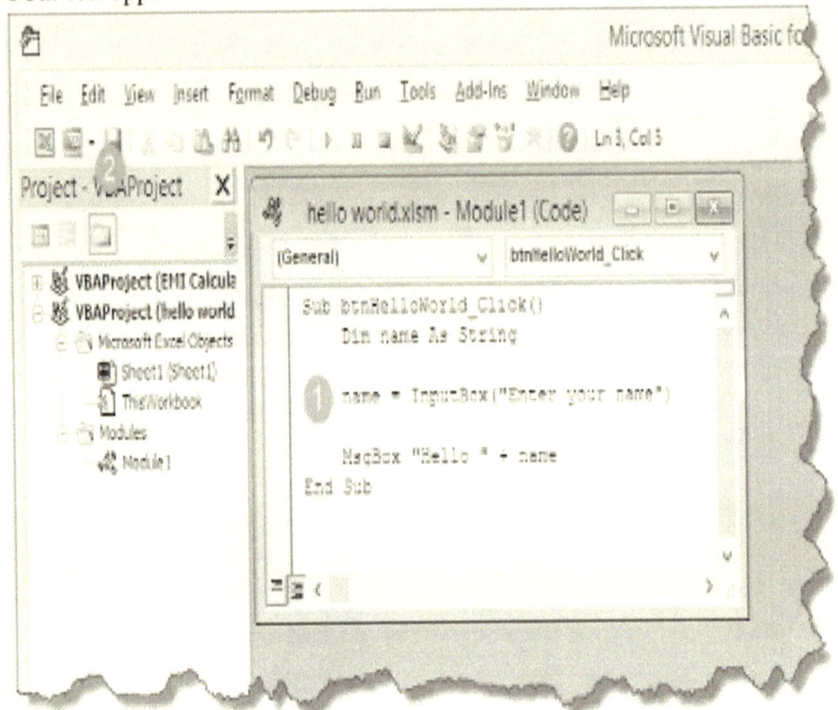

Close your code window
Right-click button 1 to edit text
Click Say Hello

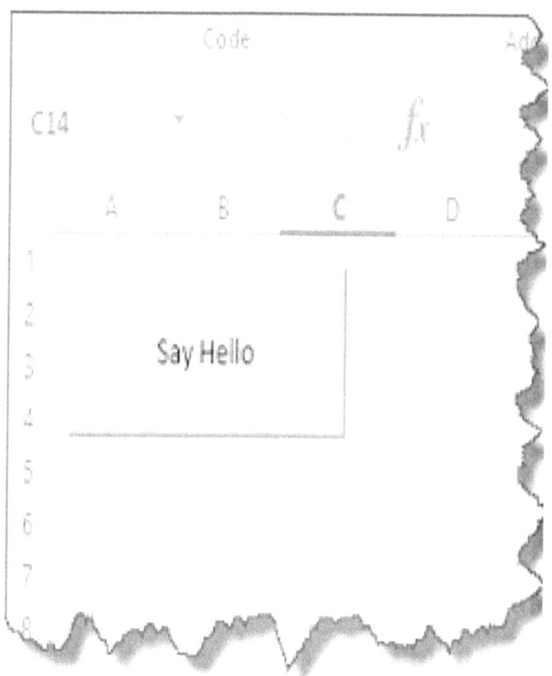

Click Say Hello
You get the following input box

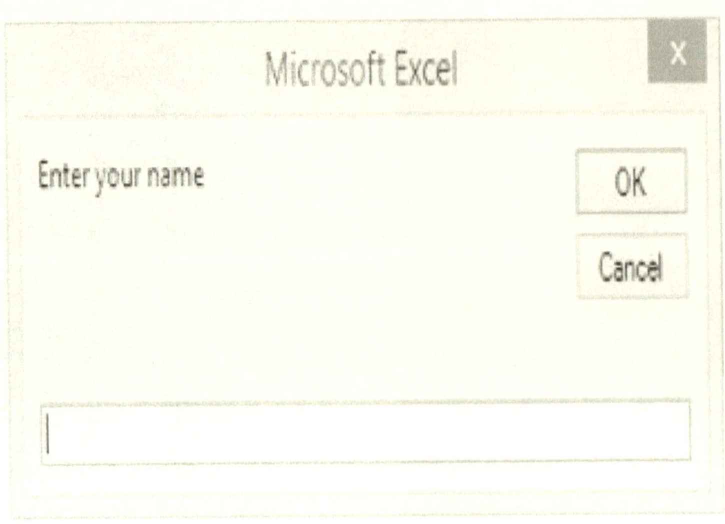

Enter your email. Jordan: Jordan
You'll get the following message box

Congratulations, you created your first **VBA** in Excel

Step by stage, Excel builds a simple EMI calculator

In this tutorial exercise, we will create a simple EMI calculation program. EMI is Equated Monthly Instalment's acronym. It's the monthly amount you pay when you get a loan. The picture below shows the EMI calculation formula.

$$EMI = P\,\frac{r(1+r)^n}{(1+r)^n - 1}$$

where:
P = principal loan amount
r = annual interest rate / 12
n = number of monthly installments

The formula above is complex and can be written in excel. Excel's good news has already taken care of the above problem. You may use PMT to calculate the above.

The PMT role follows

= PMT(rate, PV, nper)

HERE,

"Rate" is the monthly rate. It's the interest rate divided by payments per year

"Nper" is the number of payments. It is the loan term multiplied by payments per year

Present-value "PV." It's the real loan amount

Build Interface with Excel cells as shown below

	A	B	C	D	E
1	**VBA EMI Calculator**				
2					
3	Loan amount:				
4	Loan terms (years):				
5	Payment/Year:				
6	Interest:				
7					
8					
9	Calculated EMI:				
10					
11					
12					

Add command button in rows 7-8

Give the name btnCalculateEMI Click

Click Edit button

Enter the code below

Dim monthly rate Single, loan amount double, number of periods single, EMI double

Monthly rate = Range("B6").Value / Range("B5").

Loan amount = Range("B3").

Number of periods = Range("B4").Value("B5").

Emi = WorksheetFunction. Pmt(monthly rate, period number, loan amount)

Range('B9'. 'Value = emi

HERE,

"Dim monthly rate As single, ..." Dim is the keyword used to define VBA variables; the monthly rate is the variable name, single is the type of data that means the variable accepts number.

"Monthly rate = Range("B6").Value / Range("B5").Value" Range is a function used to access VBA, Range("B6) "Excel cells.
"WorksheetFunction. Pmt (...)" WorksheetFunction is the function used by all Excel functions.
The picture below shows the entire source code.

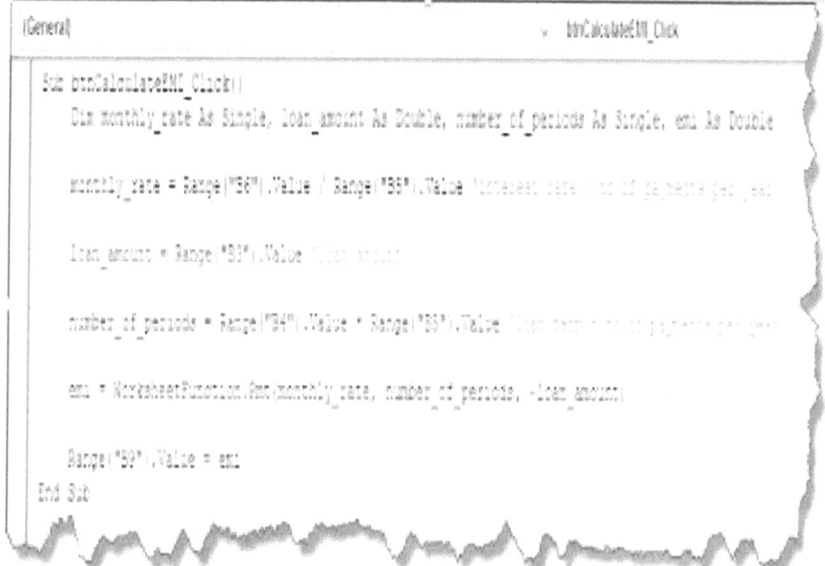

Click and close the code window
Test your program in the animated image below

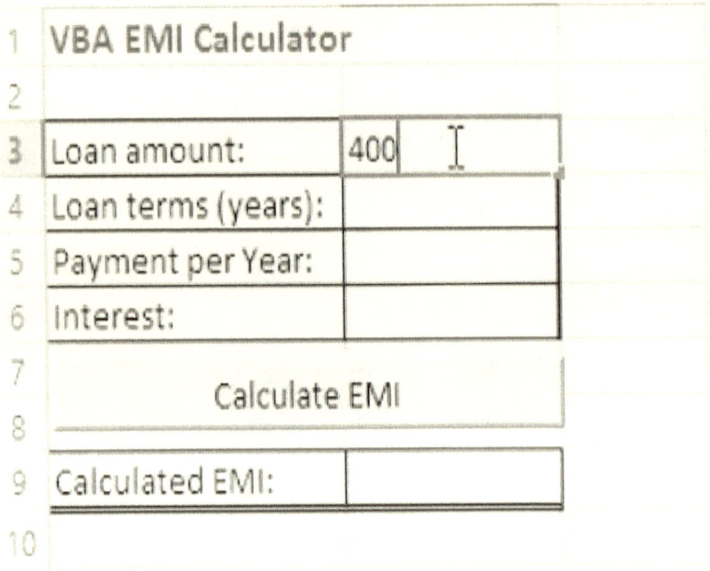

1	VBA EMI Calculator	
2		
3	Loan amount:	400
4	Loan terms (years):	
5	Payment per Year:	
6	Interest:	
7	Calculate EMI	
8		
9	Calculated EMI:	
10		

Example 2:

Step 1) Under the Developer tab, click the "Visual Basic" icon to open your VBA editor.

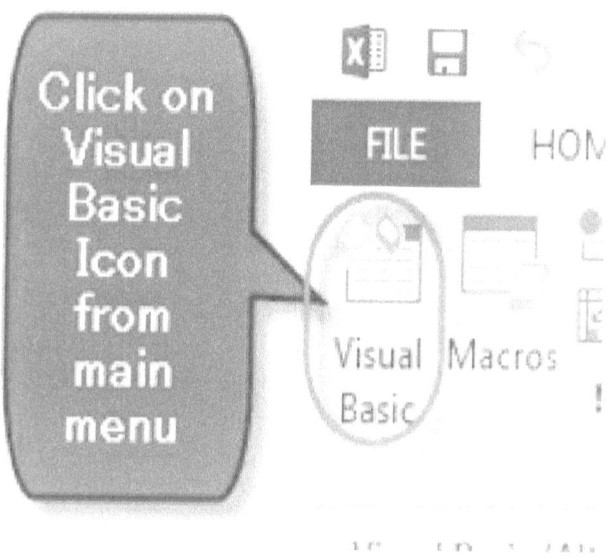

Phase 2) Open a VBA editor from where you can pick the Excel sheet to run the code. Double-click the worksheet to open the VBA editor.

It will open the folder's right-hand VBA editor. It'll look like white space.

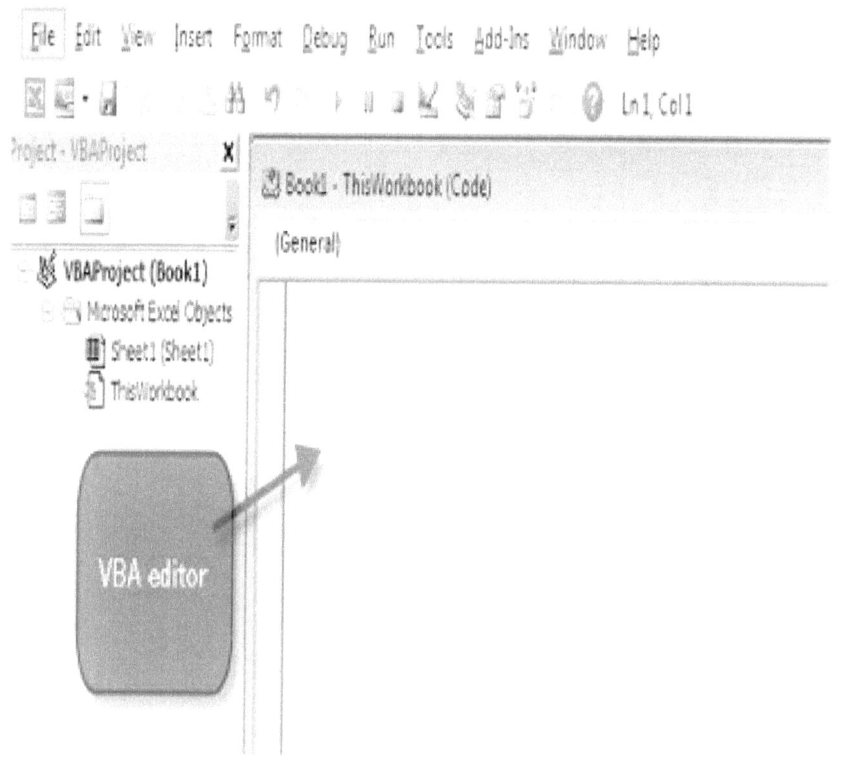

Phase 3) Here, we will see our fist VBA program. Reading and displaying our program requires an object in VBA, MsgBox object, or medium.

Write "Sub" first, then "System Name" (Guru99)

Write anything to display in MsgBox (guru99-learning is fun)

End the End Subprogram

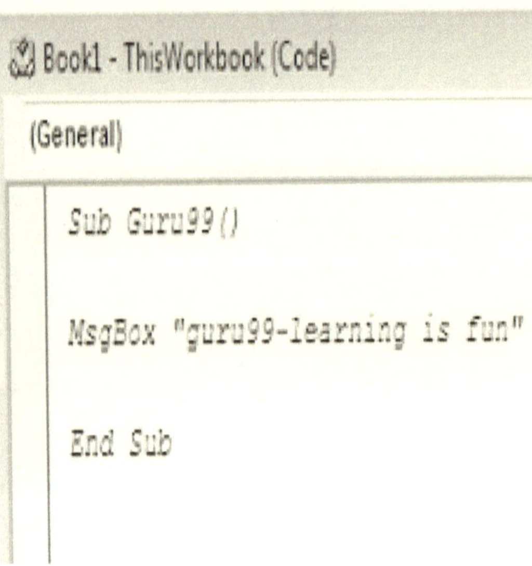

Phase 4) In the next stage, click on the green run button at the top of the editor menu to run this file.

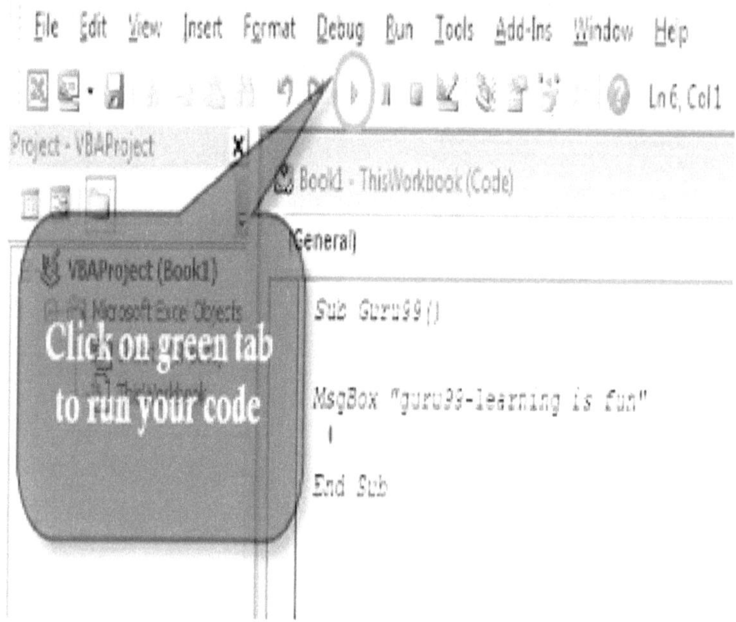

Phase 5) While running the application, another window appears. Pick the sheet where you'd want to show the program and click "Run."

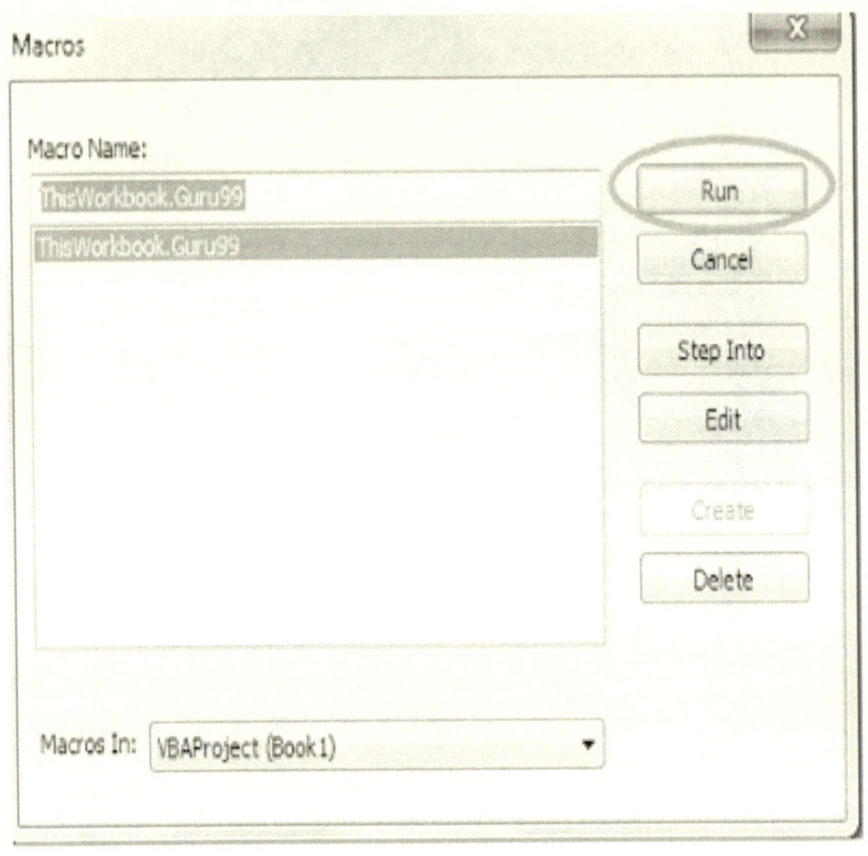

Phase 6) Press the Run button to execute the program. It shows msg in MsgBox.

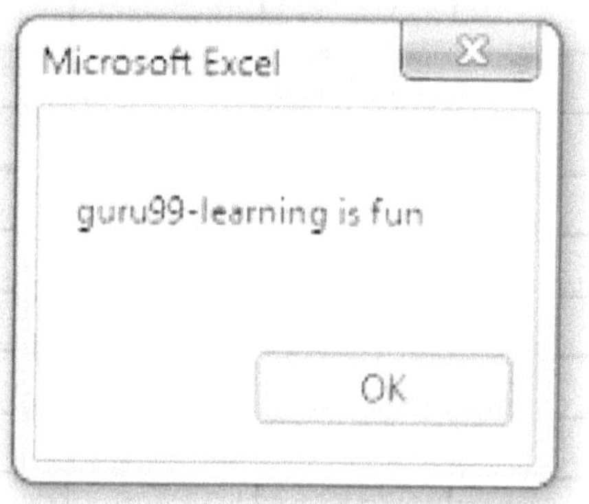

Download the above Excel Code

Summary
VBA is Visual Basic Application. It's a visual basic programming language sub-component you can use to create applications in excel. With VBA, you can still use excel's powerful features and use them in VBA.

BUSINESS MODELLING

There is a wide range of confounded meanings of budgetary demonstrating, and as far as I can tell, there is a lot of disarray around what a money related model is actually. A couple of years prior, we set up a Plum Solutions study about the mentalities, patterns, and employments of budgetary demonstrating, asking respondents, "What do you think a money related model is?" Participants were approached to put down the principal thing that rung a bell, with no exploration or an excess of pondering it. I found the reactions intriguing, diverting, and now and again rather upsetting. A few answers were excessively confounded and profoundly specialized:

■ "Portrayal of conduct/genuine perceptions through scientific methodology intended to foresee the scope of results."

■ "A lot of organized figurings, written in a spreadsheet, used to break down the operational and money related attributes of a business as well as its exercises."

■ "Tool(s) used to set and deal with a set-up of variable suppositions so as to anticipate the money related results of a chance."

■ "A build that encodes business rules, suspicions, and figurings empowering data, examination, and knowledge to be drawn out and upheld by quantitative realities."

■ "Asystemofspreadsheetsandformulastoachievethelevelofrecordkeeping and detailing required to be educated, state-of-the-art, and ready to follow funds precisely and plan for what's to come."

Some philosophical:

■ "A numerical story."

Some wrong:

■ "Anticipating riches by taking care of cash presently/contributing."

■ "It is tied in with placing information into a decent configuration."

"It is only a mega-colossal spreadsheet with extravagant recipes that are smoothed out to make your life simpler."

Some crazy:

■ "Something to do with cash and design?"

Some legitimate:

■ "I truly have no clue."

What's more, some absolute significant:

■ "An intricate spreadsheet."

There are many (regularly muddled and indulgent) definitions accessible from various sources, yet I really lean toward the vast, expansive, yet precise portrayal: "a mind-boggling spreadsheet.

." While it needs some definition, my meaning of a money related model is quite expansive. Up to a spreadsheet has money related data sources and yields, and is dynamic and adaptable, I'm glad to consider it a budgetary model! Basically, the general purpose of money related displays is that you change the information sources and the yields. This is the significant reason behind the situation and affectability examination; this is the thing that Excel, with its mathematical rationale, was made for. More often than not, a model will contain monetary data and effectively make a budgetary choice; however, not generally. Frequently it will contain a full arrangement of budget summaries: benefit and misfortune, income, and accounting report, yet not generally. As indicated by the more grave or conventional meanings of monetary demonstrating, the accompanying things would all unquestionably be delegated, budgetary models:

■ A business case that decides if to proceed with an undertaking.

■ A five-year figure indicating benefit and misfortune, income, and monetary record.

■ Pricing figurings to decide the amount to offer for another delicate.

■ Investment for a joint endeavor.

However, shouldn't something be said about different bits of examination that we proceed as a major aspect of our jobs? Will these additionally be called budgetary models? Imagine a scenario in which something doesn't contain monetary information at all.

Consider if you somehow happened to create a spreadsheet for the following purposes:

■ A genuine versus spending month to month change investigation that doesn't contain situations and for which there are no genuine suppositions recorded.

■ A hazard evaluation, where you enter the hazard, allot a probability to that chance and compute the general danger of the task utilizing likelihood calculations. This doesn't contain any budgetary yields whatsoever.

WHAT ARE THE DIFFERENCES BETWEEN A SPREADSHEET AND A FINANCIAL MODEL?

Before we proceed, let me make one thing understood: I am not inclined toward the utilization of the word spreadsheet; indeed, you'll barely think that it's utilized at all in this book.

1Ruth McKeever, Kevin McDaid, and Brian Bishop, "An Exploratory Analysis of the Impact of Named Ranges on the Debugging Performance of Novice Users."

I've regularly been asked the contrast between the two, and there is a fine line of definition between them. In a nutshell, an Excel spreadsheet is essentially the medium that we can use to make a money related model. At the most fundamental level, a budgetary model that has been worked in Excel is essentially a complex spreadsheet. By definition, a money related model is a structure that contains input information and supplies outputs. By changing the info data, we can test the consequences of these progressions on the yield results, and this kind of affectability investigation is most effortlessly done in an Excel spreadsheet. One could contend, at that point, that they are in truth something very similar; there is actually no distinction between a spreadsheet and a money related model. Others question in the event that it truly matters what we call them as long as they carry out the responsibility. All things considered, both include placing information into Excel, sorting out it, arranging, including a few equations, and making some usable yield. There are, in any case, some unobtrusive contrasts to note:

1. "Spreadsheet" is a trick all term for a data put away in Excel, including a money related model. Therefore, a spreadsheet could truly be anything: an agenda, crude information yield from a bookkeeping framework, a flawlessly spread out administration report, or a budgetary model used to assess another venture.

2. A money related model is increasingly organized. A model contains a lot of variable presumptions, inputs, yields, computations, situations, and frequently incorporates a lot of standard money related gauges, for example, benefit and misfortune, monetary record, and income, which depend on those suspicions.

3. A monetary model is dynamic. A model contains variable information sources, which, when changed, sway the yield results. A spreadsheet may be essentially a report that totals data from different sources and gathers it into a helpful introduction. It might contain a couple of recipes, for example, an aggregate at the base of a rundown of costs or normal money went through more than a year, yet the outcomes will rely upon direct contributions to those sections and lines. A budgetary model will consistently have fabricated firmness to investigate various results in every money related report dependent on changing a couple of key sources of info.

4. A spreadsheet is normally static. When a spreadsheet is finished, it regularly turns into an independent report, and no further changes are made. A budgetary model, then again, will consistently permit a client to change input factors and see the effect of these suppositions on the yield.

5. A budgetary model will utilize connections between a few factors to make money related reports, and changing any or every one of them will influence the yield. For instance, Revenue in Month 4 could be an aftereffect of Sales Price × Quantity Sold Prior Month × Monthly Growth in Quantities Sold. In this model, three components become an integral factor, and the end client

can investigate diverse blends of each of the three to see the outcomes and choose which mirrors their plan of action best.

6. A spreadsheet shows genuine chronicled information, while a monetary model contains theoretical results. A side-effect of an all-around fabricated money related model is that we can without much of a stretch use it to perform situation and affectability investigation. This is a significant result of a money related model. What might occur if loan costs increment a premise point significantly?

What amount would we be able to limit before we begin making a misfortune?

Taking everything into account, a monetary model is a mind-boggling sort of spreadsheet, while a spreadsheet is a device that can satisfy an assortment of purposes, money related models being one. The rundown of properties above can distinguish the spreadsheet as a budgetary model, yet at times we truly are discussing something very similar. Investigate the Excel documents you are utilizing. Is it true that they are dynamic, organized, and adaptable, or have you just made a static, direct info spreadsheet?

TYPES AND PURPOSES OF FINANCIAL MODELS

Models in Excel can be worked for all intents and purposes any reason—money related and nonfinancial, business-related or non-business-related—in spite of the fact that most of the models will be budgetary and business-related. Next are a few instances of models that don't catch money related data:

■ Risk the executives.
A model that catches, tracks, and reports on venture dangers, status, probability, effect, and alleviation. Restrictive organizing is regularly incorporated to make a vivid, intelligent report.

■ Project arranging.
Models might be worked to screen progress on ventures, including basic way plans and even Gantt outlines.

■ Key execution markers (KPIs) and benchmarking.
Exceed expectations is the best instrument for arranging KPI and measurements announcing. These sorts of insights are frequently pulled from a wide range of frameworks and sources, and Excel is regularly the shared factor between various frameworks.

■ Dashboards.
The prominence of dashboards has expanded in late years. The dashboard is a mixture of various measures (sometimes money related, yet regularly not), which are additionally frequently helpfully ordered and shown as graphs and tables utilizing Excel.

■ Balanced scorecards.
This assistance gives a progressively far-reaching perspective on business by concentrating on the operational, advertising, and formative execution of the association just as monetary measures. A scorecard will show estimates, for example, process execution, piece of the overall industry, or infiltration, and learning and abilities improvement, which are all effortlessly examined and showed in Excel.

UTILIZING EXCEL FOR BUSINESS AND FINANCIAL MODELING

Similarly, as with many Excel models, the greater part of these could be all the more precisely made and kept up in a reason assembled a bit of programming, however regularly the information for these sorts of reports is put away in various frameworks, and the most down to earth apparatus for arranging the information and showing it in a unique month to month report is Excel. In spite of the fact that perfectionists would not characterize these as money related models, the way that they have been fabricated should even now follow the basics of budgetary displaying best practices, for example, connecting and presumptions documentation. How we group these models is thusly just a question of semantics, and not especially significant. Returning to our unique meaning of monetary demonstrating, it is a structure (for the most part in Excel) that contains sources of info and yields and is adaptable and dynamic.

APPARATUS SELECTION

In this book, we will utilize Excel only, as that is generally proper for the sort of monetary investigation we are performing while making money related models. We frequently hear it said that Excel is the "second-best arrangement" to an issue. There is normally a superior, a progressively proficient bit of programming that will likewise give an answer; however, we frequently default to the "Swiss armed force blade" of programming, Excel, to take care of business. For what reason do numerous monetary displaying examiners use Excel solely, when they realize that better arrangements exist? At Plum Solutions, our way of thinking is additionally one of utilizing just "plain vanilla" Excel, without depending on some other outsider programming, for a few reasons:

- No extra licenses, costly use, or programming download is required.
- The product can be introduced on practically any PC.
- Little preparation is required, as most clients have some commonality with the item, which implies others will have the option to drive and comprehend your model.

■ It is a truly adaptable device. If you can see it, you can likely do it in Excel (sensibly speaking, obviously).
■ Excel can report, model, and difference for all intents and purposes of any information, from any source, across the board report.
■ But in particular, Excel is ordinarily utilized overall businesses, nations, and associations, implying that the Excel abilities you have are exceptionally transferrable.

What this last point intends to you is that on the off chance that you have great monetary demonstrating abilities in Excel, these aptitudes are going to make you more sought after, particularly in the event that you are thinking about changing ventures or jobs or finding a new line of work in another country. Actually, perhaps the best thing you can accomplish for your vocation is to improve your Excel abilities. Turning into a specialist engineer on an exclusive bit of programming is valuable, yet turning into an exceptionally talented Excel master will place you in an advantageous position all through your profession.

Exceed expectations have its impediments, obviously, and Excel's primary defeat is the straightforwardness with which clients can make blunders in their models. Hence, a huge piece of budgetary displaying best practice identifies with lessening the chance of blunders. The other issue with utilizing Excel is limit; we basically come up short on rows, especially in this period of "Enormous Data." Microsoft endeavored to keep Excel significant by presenting Power Pivot, which was free include when it was first presented in Excel 2010 and is currently local to later forms. Force Pivot can deal with a lot greater information than plain Excel, which gets around Excel's ability impediments.

Is Excel Really the Best Option?

Before bouncing straight in and making your answer in Excel, it merits looking at that as some arrangements perhaps better built-in another programming, so pause for a minute to think about your decision of programming before planning an answer. There are numerous different types of displaying programming available, and it may merit considering different alternatives other than Excel. There are additionally various Excel include is provided by outsiders that can be utilized to make money related models and perform monetary examination. The best decision relies upon the arrangement you require. The general target of a money related model decides the yield just as the computations or handling of info required by the model. Money related models are worked to give ideal, exact, and important data to aid the dynamic budgetary procedure. Subsequently, the general goal of the model relies upon the particular choices that are to be made dependent on the model's yield. As various demonstrating devices loan themselves to various arrangements or yield, before choosing a displaying apparatus, it is essential to decide unequivocally what arrangement is required dependent on the distinguished model goal.

Evaluating Modelling Tools

When the general target of the mode has been set up, a demonstrating budgetary instrument that will best suit the business prerequisites can be picked. To figure out which budgetary displaying instrument would best meet the recognized goal, the accompanying must be thought of:

■ The yield required from the model, in view of who will utilize it and the specific choices to be made.

■ The volume, multifaceted nature, type, and wellspring of info information, especially identifying with the number of reliant factors and the connections between them.

The multifaceted nature of counts or handling of contribution to be performed by the model.

■ The degree of PC education of the clients, as they ought to in a perfect world, have the option to control the model without the help of an expert.

■ The expense versus advantage set off for each displaying device.

Likewise, with all products, monetary displaying projects can either be bought as a bundle or created in-house. While buying programming as a bundle is a less expensive alternative, in an unpredictable industry, in-house improvement of explicit demonstrating programming might be important so as to give sufficient arrangements. On this occasion, one would need to draw in a certified authority to design and create proper displaying programming. Which bundle you pick relies upon the arrangement you require.

Client relationship management (CRM) information loans itself to a database, whereas something that requires complex computations, for example, those in numerous money related models, is all the more properly managed in Excel. Exceed expectations is frequently portrayed as a "bandage arrangement," since it is such an adaptable instrument, that we can use to perform practically any procedure—but not as quick or just as completely redid programming, yet it will take care of business until a drawn-out arrangement is discovered: "Spreadsheets will consistently fill the void between what a business needs today and the formally introduced frameworks."

Planning and Forecasting

Many spending plans and figures are assembled utilizing Excel, yet most significant general record frameworks have extra modules accessible that are constructed explicitly for planning and gauging. These apparatuses give a lot simpler, faster technique for making spending plans and conjectures that is less mistake inclined than utilizing formats. Notwithstanding, there are shockingly barely any organizations that have an appropriately coordinated, completely working planning and gauging framework, and the fallback arrangement is quite often Excel. There are a few reasons why numerous organizations use Excel layouts over a full planning and gauging arrangement, regardless of whether they are incorporated with their general record framework or not:

■ A full arrangement can be costly and tedious to actualize appropriately.
■ Integration with the general record framework implies an enormous interest in a specific demonstrating framework, which is hard to change later.
■ Even if a framework isn't set up, perpetually, some examination should be attempted in Excel, necessitating that at least some portion of the procedure is fabricated utilizing Excel formats.

Microsoft Office Tools:
Power Excel and Access "Plain vanilla" Excel (and by this, I mean no include

ins) is the most usually utilized device and the one we are concentrating on in this book. There are additionally other Microsoft apparatuses, both outside and inside Excel, that could likewise serve to make the arrangement, contingent upon the prerequisites. Any variant of Excel discharged from Excel 2010 onwards contains access to the apparatuses we now and then alluded to as "Power Excel." The presentation of these apparatuses was the most energizing thing to occur in the Excel world in quite a while, and it has really changed the scene for Excel clients. Note, be that as it may, that at the hour of composing, none of these devices are yet accessible for a Mac. The Power Excel suite comprises of:

- Power Query (additionally called Get and Transform)
- Power Pivot
- Power BI

Power BI is, in fact, a Power Excel device; however, it is a different work area device basically utilized for building dashboards and representations, so we won't be broadly expounding on it here.

Force Excel: Microsoft Power Query (Get and Transform) First presented as a free include in Excel 2010, Power Query is currently an inbuilt component which, in case you're utilizing Excel 2016 or later, can be gotten to by means of the Get and Transform segment of the Data Tab. It extricates information from different sources, for example, sites or different frameworks, and permits you to scrub and arrangement the information. At the point when you play out a progression of activities, this strategy can be spared, which can be over and overplayed out each time the information is invigorated. While not a demonstrating instrument, Power Query is valuable for purifying and setting up the information, prepared to use in your money related model.

Power Excel: Microsoft Power Pivot Power Pivot broadens the capacities of the PivotTable information summarization and cross-arrangement highlight by acquainting the capacity with import information from different sources. It will permit you to do things you were unable to do before in plain Excel, such as coordinating information from various sources and arranging them into a solitary report. Since it is a social database, Power Pivot makes it simple to connect together information from different sources, utilizing a straightforward "intuitive" graphical UI. Radiant as it is, we realize that plain vanilla Excel quits being so great when your information is in excess of 1,048,576 records in length, or if the information should be combined from various sources. At the point when confronted with this issue, Excel clients end up moving to an information stockroom or other, all the more remarkable programming. Microsoft has attempted to hold these clients by presenting Power Pivot, which tends to these issues with included limit and speed, yet holds the recognizable Excel interface that we as a whole know and love. As a self-administration business insight (BI) item, Power Pivot is proposed to permit clients with no specific BI or investigation preparing to create information models.

What's more, computations, sharing them either legitimately or through SharePoint archive libraries. For progressively modern clients, Power Pivot can:

■ Create your own BI arrangements without buying costly programming.

■ Manipulate huge informational indexes immediately, regardless of whether they comprise a large number of columns (Excel can't do that).

■ Construct complex imagine a scenario in which revealing frameworks with information demonstrating and information investigation articulations (DAX.

■ Link information from different sources rapidly and without any problem.

Albeit more proper for information investigation than unadulterated unique money related models, Power Pivot is absolutely worth some thought when you are building an Excel arrangement with enormous amounts of information. In the event that you find that your model has the accompanying qualities, at that point you ought to consider utilizing Power Pivot:

■ Your information contains a large number of columns, and your model is beginning to back off.

■ PivotTables or Tables are utilized widely.

■ Data should be sourced from different areas.

An extraordinary aspect concerning Power Pivot is that it is as of now part of your current Microsoft permit, so there are no extra licensing costs. There are various contrasts among renditions, and as this is a territory of fast change, I have almost certainly that the accessibility of variants and highlights may have changed when this book goes to print. The burden of utilizing Power Pivot is that in spite of the fact that you don't should be a BI authority to utilize it, figuring out how to utilize Power Pivot isn't especially clear in any event, for cutting edge clients. We offer various Power Pivot and Power BI instructional classes at Plum Solutions through our accomplices, and there are numerous recordings and online assets that can assist you with getting started in the event that you conclude that Power Pivot is the arrangement that you need. On the off chance that you are attempting to choose whether your Excel abilities are propelled enough to consider handling Power Pivot, here are a few inquiries that will assist you with determining whether you are prepared to take on Power Pivot. You should:

■ Understand and have utilized Excel's SUMIF work.

■ Have a piece of working information on sifting information in Excel (e.g., Auto or Advanced Filters).

■ Know how to manage numerous rules (e.g., SUMIFS, SUMPRODUCT, or DBASE capacities).

■ Be ready to import information from outsider databases as well as records (e.g., Access, SQL, MIS frameworks).
■ Regularly use, adapt, and modify pivot tables.

Have made determining fields in PivotTables.

■ It required a significant stretch of time to get on, yet Power Pivot has absolutely picked up in notoriety to where it has now become nearly standard among Excel clients. Microsoft has committed a lot of assets to build up the Power Pivot item, so its utilization can just keep on spreading sooner rather than later. It merits putting some time in learning it: being skillful in Power Pivot may get like having progressed Excel abilities and will be a significant expansion to your list of qualifications, and advantage your profession as an examiner.
Remember, however, that PowerPivot isn't principally a demonstrating budgetary device. It was intended with the end goal of information

examination, not budgetary displaying. Recall that—as we discussed toward the start of the part—a budgetary model, by definition, has sources of info and yields, is dynamic and adaptable; however, a model inherent PowerPivot sums up a huge amount of information into PivotTables, so, whilst certainly feasible, changing suspicions and flipping between situations is hard to do in Power Pivot.

MS Access

Since the acquaintance of Power Pivot with the Microsoft set-up of items, Access is less frequently utilized, yet it's as yet worth a notice. There is frequently some protection from utilizing Access, and it is unquestionably less well known than it used to be. Preceding the arrival of Excel 2007, Excel clients were confined to just 65,000 lines, and numerous experts and money staff utilized Access as an approach to get around this breaking point. With now over 1.1 million lines (and purportedly up to a billion lines with Power Pivot), Excel can deal with much more information, so there is less requirement for the extra column limit of Access. If you've been utilizing Access throughout the years, you may have seen that not particularly has changed in Access between adaptations. It appears that Microsoft is putting a greater amount of its endeavors into the new Power Excel as opposed to Access.

Preferences of Excel

■ Excel is remembered for most essential Microsoft Office bundles (in contrast to Access, which regularly should be bought independently), and in this manner, comes as standard on most PCs. Exceed expectations is significantly more adaptable than Access, and estimations are a lot simpler to perform.

■ It is commonly quicker to assemble an answer in Excel than in Access.

■ Excel has a more extensive information base among clients, and numerous individuals see it as increasingly natural. This implies it is faster and simpler to prepare staff in Excel.

■ It is extremely simple to make adaptable reports and diagrams in Excel.

■ Excel can report, model, and differentiation for all intents and purposes of any information, from any source, across the board document.

Exceed expectations effectively perform figurings on more than each line of information in turn, which Access experiences issues with.

Preferences of Access

■ Access can deal with a lot bigger measures of information: Excel 2003 was restricted to 65,536 lines and 256 segments, and later forms of Excel are constrained to around 1.1 million lines (1,048,576 lines, to be exact) and 16,384 segments. Access' ability is a lot bigger, and it likewise has a more prominent memory stockpiling limit.

■ Data is put away just a single time in Access, making it work all the more proficiently.
■ Data can be gone into Access by more than each client in turn.
■ Access is acceptable at crunching and controlling enormous volumes of information.

■ Due to Access's absence of adaptability, it is progressively hard for clients to make blunders.

In outline, Access is likely most usually utilized for heritage programming, databases that have been around for quite a while. On the off chance that it's fresh out of the plastic new arrangement that you need, consider Power Pivot.

Excel Add-Ins

These are programs that include discretionary orders and highlights to Excel. There are many include ins the market that has been grown explicitly for the purpose behind budgetary showing. For increasingly complex counts or preparing of information, it might be valuable to initiate or introduce at least one include ins, particularly instruments, for example, Solver, which are remembered for your MS Excel permit. Remember that different clients will most likely not have include ins empowered, so they won't have the option to perceive how your model has been made or determined. Exceed expectations include ins from all sources that can be utilized to play out an assortment of assignments that aid the demonstrating budgetary process. These include ins can be comprehensively characterized as:

- Standard Excel includes ins, for example, the Analysis ToolPak and Solver.

- Audit instruments.

- The integration connects with Excel and the general record framework.

The most regularly utilized include ins are the Analysis ToolPak and Solver, which are standard include programs that are accessible when you introduce Microsoft Office or Excel. They are remembered for the program however are crippled, of course, so on the off chance that you need to utilize them, you have to empower them. Before the arrival of Excel 2007, the best way to get to specific capacities in 2003 Excel was to download the Analysis ToolPak. Be that as it may, these capacities are presently standard in Excel, so the Analysis ToolPak is currently less regularly utilized. Different highlights in the Analysis ToolPak are apparatuses like the Data Analysis ToolPak, which has some amazing factual and building capacities not ordinarily utilized in budgetary displaying.

WHAT IS FINANCIAL MODELLING?

This is a very helpful, however very propelled apparatus for ideal computing qualities in money related displaying. Reviews include ins for Excel are utilized to guarantee the precision of information and estimations inside a spreadsheet or exercise manual. They can rapidly distinguish recipe mistakes by taking a gander at conflicting equations, looking at variants, and getting to the base of complex named ranges. There are a few custom include ins accessible both from Microsoft and different gatherings that will encourage exactness by performing equation examinations, point of reference/subordinate analysis, worksheet analysis, and affectability announcing. While they can help with checking for equation blunders, there are numerous different kinds of mistakes that can undoubtedly be overlooked, and using these add-ins can give a misguided feeling that all is well and good. Joining include ins permit data from the money related announcing framework to be moved into Excel for additional examination, or information put away in Excel to be moved into the revealing monetary framework. These are frequently utilized with the end goal of:

■ Transferring data from the general record framework into Excel for the reasons for detailing and examination. Numerous administration reports are worked in Excelandextractup-to-date information straightforwardly from the general record framework into the reports.

■ Loading data as diary sections once more into the general ledger framework. Information is frequently controlled in Excel and afterward stacked into the general record as a diary. For instance, if a receipt should be part of various divisions dependent on the headcount portion, this figuring may be done in Excel, split to offices in the diary, and stacked into the general record framework.

The more complex a monetary model is, the more costly it is to keep up. It is, thusly, best to utilize a model with the least conceivable degree of refinement expected to give a particular arrangement. Consequently, buying a product bundle, if it can convey the ideal arrangement, maybe fitting. When the choice has been made to buy a product bundle, it must be resolved which bundle will give the best arrangement as specific arrangements might be better given by specific programming bundles. There are numerous types of programming and Excel include ins the market that can be utilized to make budgetary models. Nonetheless, given that it can convey a satisfactory arrangement, we suggest utilizing plain Excel, as it is anything but difficult to utilize, and no additional licenses, preparing, or programming downloads are required. On the off chance that extra usefulness is required, Excel includes ins might be thought of

WHAT ARE SKILLS YOU REQUIRE TO BE A GOOD FINANCIAL MODELLER?

When you choose your budgetary models are not on a par with they ought to be, would it be a great idea to promptly take a progressed Excel course? While this is useful, there's significantly more to money related displaying than being acceptable at Excel! While considering the abilities that make up a decent monetary modeler, we have to separate between theoretical displaying, which is to have a comprehension of the exchange, business, or item being demonstrated, and spreadsheet designing, which is the portrayal of that calculated model in a spreadsheet. Spreadsheet abilities are sensibly simple to discover, however, a modeler who can comprehend the idea of the motivation behind the model and make an interpretation of it into a reasonable, succinct, and all around organized model is a lot rarer. Individuals who need to manufacture a budgetary model some of the time think they have to turn out to be either an Excel super-client or a bookkeeping star who knows each all through bookkeeping rules. I'd contend you need a mix of both, just as various different aptitudes, including some business sound judgment!

Spreadsheet and Technical Excel Skills
It's simple for money related modelers to get stalled in the specialized Excel parts of their model, lose it with complex equations, and not center around the key significant level, best-practice systems, for example, blunder checking techniques and model pressure testing. Exceed expectations is an unfathomably incredible tool, and basically, no single Excel user will have the need or want to use the majority of the use this program offers. Likewise, with most programming, the 80/20 principle applies: 80 percent of clients utilize just 20 percent of the highlights, albeit some would contend that 95 percent of Excel clients utilize just 5 percent of the highlights! In any case, there are those chosen few who see each all through Excel, each and every capacity and work out how to do for all intents and purposes anything in Excel. Do you have to have this degree of Excel aptitude to turn into a decent budgetary modeler?
Lamentably, having extraordinary programming aptitudes doesn't generally help with regards to applying them to a particular region of business. Understand that Excel is utilized in a few limits, so being an Excel super-

client doesn't consequently mean you'll be an excessively money related modeler. The best monetary models are clear, all around organized, adaptable, and dynamic; they are not generally the greatest and most confused models that utilization the most progressive apparatuses and capacities. A considerable lot of the best money related models utilize just Excel's center usefulness. Having said that, to be a decent money related modeler, you do need to know Excel extraordinarily well. Those individuals who keep up that you needn't bother with great Excel abilities to be a budgetary modeler are typically those with powerless Excel aptitudes. You ought to construct an amazing model utilizing basic and direct apparatuses in light of the fact that you've decided to make your model understood and simple to follow, not on the grounds that that is all you realize how to do. You don't need to be a super-client—the 99th percentile in Excel information —however, you should absolutely be better than expected. A complex money related model may utilize includes in Excel that the ordinary client doesn't have the foggiest idea. The best budgetary model will consistently utilize the arrangement that is the least difficult instrument to finish the undertaking (as basic as could be expected under the circumstances and as mind-boggling as fundamental, right?), so the more comfortable you are with the devices accessible in Excel, the simpler it will be. An exhibit equation or a large scale may be the best way to accomplish what you have to accomplish, yet a less difficult arrangement likely could be—and regularly is—prevalent. You may likewise need to dismantle another person's model, which utilizes complex devices, and it's extremely hard to control a cluster recipe or a large scale in the event that you've never observed one. Along these lines, on the off chance that you are thinking about a vocation as a money related modeler (as I expect you seem to be), improving your Excel information is a brilliant spot to begin.

Industry Knowledge
An awesome aspect regarding money related displaying is that it is pertinent across such huge numbers of various enterprises. Great monetary demonstrating abilities will consistently stand you in good stead, regardless of which industry or nation you are working in. Money related displaying experts or generalists will likely work in a wide range of ventures during their professions and have the option to manufacture models for various items and administrations. They will likely not be specialists in the complexities of

every industry, notwithstanding, and that is the reason it's significant for a monetary demonstrating generalist to counsel cautiously with the topic master for the data sources, presumptions, and rationale of the money related model. Try not to be reluctant to pose parcels and heaps of inquiries if the subtleties are not totally clear. All things considered, the individual who has charged the model hasn't really considered the means, sources of info, suppositions, and even what the yields ought to resemble until you pose the correct inquiry. Money related demonstrating specialists are exceptionally mindful so as to move obligation regarding the suspicions to the end-user, which is an entirely reasonable game-plan. The individual structure the model is frequently not the person who has authorized it or the individual who is really utilizing it. Model developers are frequently not excessively acquainted with the item or even the association, and they can't (and ought not) assume liability for the sources of info. For instance, when fabricating an evaluating model, the modeler needs to comprehend the item and how the expenses and income work. Involvement in administrative limitations will assist the modeler with understanding the premise of guideline and its components(e.g., cost building squares, cost record, income top, weighted normal value top, greatest costs, and so on.). Comprehension of monetary ideas, for example, productive cost estimation, return on and of an administrative resource base, working expenses, and working capital, since quite a while ago run versus short-run peripheral expenses, and normal expenses, are different instances of industry information that is helpful for the money related modeler.

INSTANCES OF INDUSTRY KNOWLEDGE

- Regulatory imperatives.
- Industry gauges.
- The maximum value that can be charged for a specific thing.

Bookkeeping Knowledge

Components, for example, fiscal summaries, income, and assessment counts, can be a significant part of numerous monetary models. Proficient bookkeepers realize each and every bookkeeping rule and law there is, yet this positively doesn't, by definition, make them great monetary modelers. In the event that a profoundly gifted bookkeeper constructed a money related model, you would figure that the calculations, layout, and structure of the fiscal summaries will be 100 percent right, yet will they be connected appropriately? On the off chance that you change a portion of the sources of info, does the accounting report despite everything balance? Once in a while, not! A decent bookkeeper or even somebody qualified who has a Master's certificate in the applied fund, for instance, probably won't be comfortable with all the specialized displaying apparatuses, regardless of whether the person is an equipped Excel client. Likewise, with the other demonstrating aptitudes, you needn't bother with a top degree of bookkeeping information to fabricate a money related model. Truth be told, money related models are regularly moderately direct from a bookkeeping outlook. You positively shouldn't be a certified bookkeeper to turn into a monetary modeler, albeit a decent comprehension of bookkeeping and information on account unquestionably makes a difference. There are a few circumstances where industry information and bookkeeping are required for monetary displaying. For instance, in assembling or, especially, in the oil and gas industry, the modeler has to know whether FIFO (first-in, first-out) or LIFO (rearward in, first out) bookkeeping is being utilized, as this bigly affects how the stock is being demonstrated. A money related modeler who has never worked in these enterprises might not have ever known about FIFO and LIFO, and would most likely have no clue about how to demonstrate them.

INSTANCES OF ACCOUNTING KNOWLEDGE

- How is a benefit and misfortune explanation organized?
- How would I develop an income estimate from my model?
- How would I transform capital consumption into a deterioration cost?

Business Knowledge

A modeler with wide-running business experience is well prepared to test for the realities and suppositions that are basic for building a money related model. This is likely the most troublesome aptitude to instruct, as it's most effortlessly got by working in an administration job. Business discernment is especially significant when charging, structuring, and deciphering a money related model. While making the model, the modeler needs to think about the reason for the model. What does the model need to let us know? Realizing the ideal result will help with the model's form, structure, and sources of info. In the event that, for instance, we are building a valuing model, we have to think about the ideal result—normally, the value we have to charge in order to accomplish a specific overall revenue. What is an adequate edge? What expenses would it be a good idea for us to incorporate? What cost will the market bear? Modelers ought to likewise have a comprehension of financial ideas, for example, proficient expenses and how these are determined, a normal profit for an asset base, operating expenses, and working capital, or since quite a while ago run versus short-run peripheral expenses. Obviously, the responses to these inquiries can be acquired from others, yet a modeler with great negotiating prudence will have an intrinsic feeling of how a model ought to be assembled, and what is the most legitimate plan and format to accomplish the important outcomes.

INSTANCES OF BUSINESS KNOWLEDGE

■ What is the expense of capital, and how does that influence a business case?

■ Which numbers are significant?

■ What does the inner pace of return mean, and what is a worthy rate?

Tasteful Design Skills

This is a zone that numerous modelers and examiners battle with, as aesthetics basically don't fall into place easily for left-mind scholars like us. We are, for the most part, so worried about precision and usefulness that we neglect to understand that the model looks—and I'm not going to dance around the issues here—revolting! Despite the fact that it's only a straightforward matter of taking as much time as necessary when organizing, the vast majority of us. Research shows that clients place more prominent confidence in models with stylish arranging than those without, so one of the quickest and least demanding approaches to give your model validity is to just put in no time flat on the hues, textual style, format, and plan. Some stylish designing is basic for the usefulness and to keep away from the mistake, yet for the most part, it includes believability and makes your model simpler to work with. Models can become complex rapidly, and without a very much arranged plan, they can be muddled. Some essential parts of a model ought to be a spreadsheet, directions, and obviously marked sources of info, yields, functions, and results. For very long and complex models with numerous sheets, a hyperlinked chapter by chapter guide is likewise an important expansion to enable the client to explore the model.

Correspondence and Language Skills

This is additionally a territory that we analytical, financially orientated individuals are not in every case great at. A few experts like to bolt themselves away, taking a shot at spreadsheets without speaking with others. In the event that this is your tendency, then you may need to consider whether budgetary displaying is a decent professional decision for you, in light of the fact that there is an astounding measure of human collaboration required for most money related modelers.

■ Assumptions approval.

So as to pick up a purchase in from partners, the key suspicions and data sources regularly should be conveyed verbally or recorded as a hard copy. Individuals in different pieces of the business ought to be associated with a request to check the exactness and fittingness of contributions for consideration in a model. Partners will regularly inquiry the suppositions or the manner in which they have been utilized and give very significant understanding of modelers (especially for a specialist or modeler with little industry or item information). Playing out this errand well is a basic advance in the displaying procedure.

UTILIZING EXCEL FOR BUSINESS AND FINANCIAL MODELING

■ Data gathering.

There are some demonstrating ventures where additional time is spent assembling and examining information than really fabricating the model. Holders of data can be monitored about offering access to information now and then unreasonably, however regularly; this is on the grounds that they've had awful encounters before. This can happen when somebody gives assesses in private and later finds that those numbers have been utilized in financial plans or different archives to which they are considered responsible. Along these lines, individuals can be justifiably hesitant about giving information when mentioned to a specially appointed venture, for example, a monetary model.

A modeler with good communication skills will be able to dig, delve, and coax the information out of them!

■ Presentation skills.

Senior administration, when favoring a venture, frequently need to catch wind of the money related ramifications of the task from the individual who really manufactured the model; thus, modelers are here and there required to introduce the key results to a board or official advisory group. Having the option to distill a 30MB, very unpredictable money related model that contains 20 tabs and took you a month and a half to work, into three PowerPoint slides and a six-minute outline introduction, can be a serious test!

■ Client aptitudes.

Irrespective of whether you're an expert or an in-house employee, working admirably with clients is a useful skill. Even in-house modelers have clients; every individual you work with or for ought to be viewed as a customer and rewarded with similar regard and thought as if they were taking care of your tab. In these collaborations with others, monetary modelers must show trust in their model. Manufacture the model as well as could be expected.

Utilize best practices, check for mistakes, and follow a decent and sensible manner of thinking so you can do it in a manner that oozes outright certainty when you introduce or talk about your mode. This reduces your model's accuracy, usefulness, and validity issues. Be frank about your model's fallibility and known flaws (let's face it, no model is perfect), but be sure you've built it to best practice standards within time, data, or scope limitations. This will increase the credibility of your model, build your reputation within your company, and, of course, enhance your career!

Numeracy Skills
Monetary models, obviously, have a huge numerical part, and people with great numeracy abilities are most appropriate to them. Strong scientific aptitudes can be especially valuable in mistake checking and sense-checking. The capacity to make unpleasant gauges rapidly implies they will have the option to spot blunders all the more without any problem. In the event that we sell 450 units at $800 each, will our business income be $3.6 million, or $360,000? On the off chance that we've made a figuring blunder, the numerate modeler will get the slip-up significantly more rapidly.

The modeler with numerical fitness will likewise have a gut feel for separating between basic suppositions that need further check, and information that is inconsequential or irrelevant to the model. The less numerate modeler should test it physically, and will most likely wind up with a similar outcome; however, it will basically take a longer time. General numeracy is an ability that is hard to instruct, and one that can without much of a stretch be pursued for in the enlistment system. Experience working with models after some time can definitely improve these abilities, as the modeler who is less numerate will learn approaches to repay through mistake testing, and these procedures will get gained intrinsic propensities.

Capacity to Think Logically
Modeling is often like programming, and complex reason ought to be deciphered into the language of Excel with the goal that the program can comprehend and make the modeler's ordinary results. For instance, on the off chance that we need to show worth, however just if the cell being tried is, later on, we would vocalize it by saying: "Show me the worth, yet just if the test cell is more noteworthy than or equivalent to the present date." The way that we have to make an interpretation of this into Excel's language is to utilize the recipe IF(test_cell>=today, value, ◆◆)
The rationale is additionally basic for the model format, structure, and the utilization of suppositions in estimations. The issue of timing in yearly

models is one that I regularly use while showing rationale in my preparation workshops. On the off chance that we are assessing the income for another protection item, and the supposition that will be that we obtain 30,000 clients consistently, we can't expect income for the full 30,000 clients, as not every one of them will start on the absolute first day of Year 1. Clients will be procured continuously consistently, so we have to take a normal so as to figure income. This is a case of how it is exceptionally simple to misunderstand rationale and overestimate income by a significant sum. The rationale is one of those investigative abilities that are hard to educate, however, modelers who have made a rationale blunder (like the one delineated above) gain rapidly from their slip-ups and are very mindful so as to utilize clear, all around reported rationale for others to follow and check.

THE "PERFECT" FINANCIAL MODELER

By and large, most modelers have probably a portion of the previously mentioned abilities, and on occasion, it is important to counsel authorities so as to make an effective money related model. Having perused the segment on the aptitudes that you should be a decent money related modeler, you ought to have a genuinely smart thought about which zones you are inadequate in. When you have recognized these zones, you can work to improve them and liaise with different experts to guarantee that your model isn't missing because of your shortcomings. What monetary modelers bring to the table is a mix of abilities. In any case, they know Excel okay to have the choice to pick the least troublesome and most practical apparatus to assemble a model. They can make a PivotTable, exhibit recipe, or full scale (however, just when essential, obviously), utilize a basic or complex settled equation, and pick the best-specialized apparatus to perform situation examination. They also understand all the important business and bookkeeping standards. By the day's end, the asset report needs to adjust, and the closure money on your income explanation needs to bind to the accounting report, for instance. The ideal financial modeler brings a unique combination of skills that neither an Excel guru nor an accounting whiz possesses. He or she understands the sensitivity and connections between factors, how changes in sources of info will affect the results, and how this should be displayed in Excel. A budgetary modeler can likewise make a stride back and acknowledge what a definitive objective of the model ought to be. Is it true that we are building a model for in-house use, or to present to financial specialists? Do we need a valuation, a fluctuation examination, a pleasant synopsis, or a point by point month-by-month profit and loss report? The financial modeler can take information, build an Excel model that is, in fact, right from a bookkeeping stance, set up the model, and at last, reflect what the business is hoping to accomplish.

Prior to propelling in to fabricate a model, it's imperative to consider the model plan, structure, configuration, and orchestrating. An especially thought out structure and clear endeavor plan can have a colossal effect on the quality and achievement of the displaying venture.

Configuration can some of the time be the most troublesome piece of building a money related model and, from experience, one of the hardest to instruct and learn. The most ideal approach to create structure abilities is to basically evaluate others' models, observing what works and doesn't, and afterward applying it to your own models. Indeed, even the easiest models can get mind-boggling if ineffectively planned, and a very much structured model will so clearly sense that it will just represent itself with no issue. It's truly simple to simply make a plunge and begin assembling a model without considering the ramifications of the plan. It is anything but a poorly conceived notion to invest some energy pondering the design before you begin. The design and structure of the model identify with the look and feel of the model and how clients explore through the model. The accompanying models plot several unique difficulties you may run over when planning the design of a model.

Pragmatic Example 1: Assumptions Layout Let's say you are making an elevated level 5-year gauge. We have 15,065 clients in 2020, and we are anticipating that that number should increment by 5 percent consistently. On the off chance that you set up your model as appeared in Layout Option 1 in Figure 2.1, with just a single development supposition, you're a lot of limited to a solitary contribution for the development number. In the event that we change the plan of the estimations by including numerous information suspicion cells, and change the equation only a bit, we are making our model significantly more adaptable and helpful in the long haul. Along these lines, in the event that we choose to change the development number for every year, we won't have to change any of our equations later on, and our model is significantly more powerful and less inclined to blunder. Obviously, Layout Option 2 is somewhat progressively mind-boggling yet is increasingly practical for the client. This model exhibits the consistent equalization that a modeler needs to keep up among usefulness and straightforwardness when assembling a money related model.

Handy Example 2: Summary Categorisation
Masterminding items to show into classifications in a model is another conceivably troublesome model format issue. Suppose you're making an estimating model for some promoting items. You have print promotions and computerized advertisements, and these are both parts of Display and Text Only. The question to be asked is, would it be advisable to show the yield of your model? The model is progressively succinct yet shows less detail, so it

truly relies upon how much detail you need to show your client. This correlation exhibits the consistent equalization that a modeler needs to keep up among detail and succinctness when assembling a monetary model.

THE GOLDEN RULES FOR MODEL DESIGN

There are a couple of decides for the model structure that ought to be followed when planning the format of a model. Most experienced modelers will follow these naturally, as they are commonly the presence of mind.

Separate inputs, estimates, and tests, where obviously possiblename which areas of the model contain sources of info, figurings, and results. They can be on discrete worksheets or separate places on a given worksheet, however, ensure that the client knows precisely what each area is for. Shading coding can help with guaranteeing that each area is unmistakably characterized. See the imminent segment entitled "The Workbook Anatomy of a Model" for more conversation on whether it is consistently handy to isolate these areas.

USING EXCEL FOR BUSINESS AND FINANCIAL MODELLING

Utilize Each Column for the Same Purpose
This is especially significant for models, including time arrangement. For instance, in a period arrangement model, realizing that marks are in Column B, unit information in Column C, consistent qualities in Column D, and computations in Column E makes it a lot simpler when altering a recipe physically.

Utilize One Formula for every Row or Column
This forms the basis of the best-practice principle whereby formulas are kept consistent utilizing supreme, relative, and blended referencing. Keep recipes reliable when in a square of information, and never change an equation part of the way through.

Allude to the Left or more
The model should peruse coherently, similar to a book, implying that it ought to be perused from left to right and start to finish. Counts, data sources, and yields should stream intelligently to evade roundabout referencing. Know that there are times when left-to-right or start to finish information stream can struggle to some degree effortlessly of utilization and introduction, so utilize sound judgment when structuring the design. By following this training, we can abstain from having computations connect everywhere throughout the sheet, which makes it harder to check and update. Exceed expectations will likewise figure all the more rapidly on the off chance that you construct equations along these lines since it ascertains left to right, and through and through, so in addition to the fact that it makes your model simpler to follow, it will compute all the more effectively.

Utilize Multiple Worksheets
Maintain a considerable distance from the compulsion in putting everything on one sheet. Particularly when squares of estimations are the equivalent, utilize separate sheets for those that must be rehashed to dodge the need to look over the screen.

Incorporate Documentation Sheets

A documentation sheet—where suspicions and source information are obviously spread out—is a crucial component of any financial model. A cover sheet shouldn't be confused for a suppositions sheet. A model can never have a lot of documentation!

Configuration issues
Here are four key issues you have to consider before you start a model:

1. Time arrangement.

Most money related models incorporate a period arrangement component, and most of these will be month to month, quarterly, or yearly. It's critical to get this privilege from the beginning, as it's a lot simpler, to sum up, a month to month model up to a yearly premise than it is to part a yearly model down to a month to month premise!

2. Information assortment. Frequently, most of the time is spent not in building a model, but instead gathering, deciphering, investigating, and controlling information to place into the model. For instance, you could be building a yearly model for your organization's fiscal year, which goes from 1st July to 30th June; however, the review information you've gathered and need to incorporate is for the period 1st January to 31st December. If you have access to the crude information on a month to month premise, you'll have the option to control the information with the goal that it's exact—or, more than likely you'll have to extrapolate.

3. Model reason. Consider what it is that you need the model to do. What yields do you anticipate that the model should appear? The result that you need the model to show will enormously impact the plan of the model. For instance, in a business case or task assessment model, the result that we are moving in the direction of is the net present worth (NPV), and so as to get that, we need income, for which we need a benefit and shortfall articulation, and this at that point decides how we construct the model.

4. Model crowd. Who will utilize your model later on? On the off chance that it's just for your utilization, no compelling reason to make it extravagant, yet most models are worked for others to utilize. Provided that this is true, you should make your model as easy to understand as could be expected under

the circumstances, and obviously characterize which cells are input factors and which can't be changed. If you anticipate that clients should have restricted information on Excel, the model should be as easy to use as could reasonably be expected.

THE WORKBOOK ANATOMY OF A MODEL

Ordinarily, modelers will work from back to front when fabricating their model. The yield, or the part they need the watcher or client to see, will be at the front, figurings will go in the center, and source information and presumptions ought to go at the back. Figure 2.5 shows a case of what your tabs in an all-around organized model may resemble. Like the official outline, a board paper, or other report, the initial not many pages ought to contain what easygoing watchers need to see initially. In the event that they need additional data, they can delve further into the model except if a model is little, there ought to be a committed tab worksheet for each significant part of the model. While in no way, shape, or form a prescriptive rundown, coming up next is a case of what may be remembered for every tab.

■ Coversheet.
The coversheet contains many details about the model.Whether or not a spreadsheet is fundamental is an issue for banter; one can incorporate (however isn't restricted to) subtleties, for example,

■ A log of switches and updates to the model with the date, creator, changed details, and their effect on the yield of the model. This is significant for adaptation control.

■ Flowchart of the model structure.

■ Table of substance.

■ Instructions on the most reliable method to utilize the model.

■ The motivation behind the model for which it ought to be utilized.

■ Disclaimers with regards to the constraints of the model, legitimate obligation, and admonitions.

■ Global or key presumptions basic to the utilization of the model.

■ Input sheet.
This is actually the main spot where hardcoded information is permitted.

There might be at least one information sheets if there are plentiful measures of information; however the information ought to be spread out in consistent squares, for instance: utilization information, WACC information, resources and deterioration information, swelling and lists, evaluating and duties, suppositions, and constants, (for example, charge rate, rebate rates, concession rates).

■ Output, synopsis, and situation sheets. These present the ultimate results. They may likewise contain drop-down situation boxes, turn catches or checkboxes that permit the clients of the model to create their own yields. Tables and outlines summing up the yields ought to be set up so that they can without much of a stretch be printed or used to create reports. Guarantee that these can without much of a stretch be printed straightforwardly from the model, or duplicated or connected to different projects, for example, Word or PowerPoint.

■ Calculation or functions sheets. Split the count sheets legitimately and afterward, inside each sheet, set them up reliably. In the event that computation sheets are part, guarantee that the design and organizing are as predictable as conceivable overall sheets.

■ Error check sheet. This sheet contains associations with all mix-up checks in the model. Mistake checks ought to be acted in the figuring segment; however, an outline of all goof checks in a solitary zone suggests that once the model is being utilized, the modelers can rapidly verify whether any of the mistake checks have been activated.

Workbook Anatomy Issues
Matters to consider when designing the layout and structure of the model include:
■A spreadsheet.
Is a spreadsheet important? It's not completely basic, yet it is commonly accepted practice to place one in. I would say, spreadsheets and guidance pages are once in a while utilized. If you decide not to incorporate a spreadsheet, ensure that the model contains express directions in regards to activity, reason, presumptions, source information, and disclaimers.

■ Input and yield areas.

Ought to there be a devoted info sheet, or should the sources of info and yields be contained in one sheet? Many demonstrating experts keep up that information sources, yields, and estimations must be plainly isolated; however, this isn't generally handy. For the most part, bigger models ought to have a devoted info sheet, while littler models may show data sources and yields on a similar sheet. Nevertheless, if you've made an enormous model with sources of info and yields on various sheets, and afterward need to play out a situation investigation utilizing an information table, you'll have to move the data sources and yields to a similar sheet. For instance, in a little model that takes inputs and produces basic tables of yield information and diagrams in reports, the modeler may arrange the sheet to have a square of contribution at the highest point of the worksheet with the counts and outlines legitimately underneath. You may consider parting the graphs and proportion computations into discrete worksheets to dodge the worksheet getting excessively long and clumsy.

■ Calculation association.
Should figurings be on one or numerous sheets? Contingent upon the size of the model, all computations could be contained inside one worksheet, spread more than a few worksheets, or even spread more than a few exercise manual records. In the event that the estimations become long and befuddling, it bodes well to part them into intelligent segments. For instance, they can be part by kind of administration, clients, budgetary tables, topographical areas, or business sections.

■ Color coding.
In a situation where you choose to utilize shading (and I suggest that you do, or, more than likely, your model will look really exhausting), ensure that the hues you use are reliable. For example, if African areas are yellow, Europe is blue, and Asia is pink, ensure that you utilize those equivalent hues each time numbers for Africa, Europe, and Asia are shown. These hues ought to be predictable in estimations in your model, show tables, and outlines. A few organizations have standard shading coding, yet in the event that your organization doesn't, you should seriously mull over building up a norm. You could consider including a shading code key on the cover page. Using predefined styles (found on the Home tab) can make shading coding extremely brisk and simple. The following are some ordinarily utilized shading codes that are bolstered by the inbuilt styles in Excel that you may

consider embracing in your organization:

- Blue text style and beige foundation for input cells.

- Pink or dark for blunder checks.

- Green or orange for outer connections.

Organizing could be very tedious, and utilizing of styles is a period cognizant method of making unsurprising structuring. Figure 2.6 demonstrates where to discover the Styles menu on the Home tab.

Utilize a twofold outskirt to demonstrate that the computations change. In Figure 2.7, the twofold line shows that the recipe isn't predictable over the column. Numerous organizations have their predefined shading coding stacked as style formats, which guarantees consistency in shading coding in monetary models.

PROJECTPLANNING YOUR MODEL

While preparing is significant for effective demonstrating, it is ridiculous to expect that a definite undertaking plan can be made preceding beginning to assemble it. Frequently the modelers don't have a lot of thought of the size and extent of a model until they get in and begin chipping away at it.

To what extent Does it Take to Build a Financial Model?
Regardless of whether you are an expert structure, a model for a customer, or an inside modeler, you or the individual who has dispatched the model form will, justifiably, need to realize to what extent it will take. The appropriate response is rarely direct. Similarly, as with numerous different errands, it truly relies upon how much time you have (and there will never be sufficient opportunity), and how much detail the clients need. The additional time you have, the better the model will be! A few models could take many long periods of devoted work, yet it is additionally conceivable to put together a significant level model in a day or two. In a significant level model, the presumptions would likely be just gauges, as you won't have had the opportunity to approve them with partners, and the counts will be entirely unpleasant. You additionally probably won't have much in the method of extravagant hues, organizing, drop-down boxes, or checkboxes, yet the numbers should at present be sensibly precise.

Building a Model Under Pressure
It's a basic point to recall that in any event, when under colossal time tension, the modeler ought to never settle on great work rehearses. Indeed, even in an elevated level model, accepted procedures ought to be clung to, and right marking and documentation of suspicions ought to be kept up. Thus, there should be surprisingly little contrast in the base numerical result between a significant level model that takes a couple of days, and a point by point model that could take months. Whenever in a hurry, restorative highlights, for example, those appeared underneath, can be precluded. Time allowing, the nitty-gritty model may appear:

■ Detailed suspicions documentation, approved by key task partners.

■ Scenarios and affectability investigation, utilizing drop-down boxes,

checkboxes, or information tables.
- Table of substance or route devices.
- Colors and designing, restrictive organizing, and inclusion of organization logos.
- Output synopsis and nitty-gritty investigation of yield.

Time ought to be spent on brisk successes. Utilize your judgment to invest your energy in counts that are material to the model. Try not to sit around idly on approving minor presumptions that are not material to the result of the model.

MODEL LAYOUT FLOWCHARTING

In view of an underlying idea conversation of the issue, modelers can outline the structure of the model and how it will show up at the necessary yields. For models that will be seen by outside gatherings and huge or increasingly complex models, a flowchart outline that maps the model's structure and how it tackles the issue is basic. In addition to the fact that this helps in building the model, it likewise helps clients of the model to more readily comprehend the model's rationale, plan, and reason, and can be utilized as an introduction device while clarifying the model. Setting aside the effort to plan the design and structure of the model is especially useful if there is a vulnerability about what the model needs to cover, regarding both broadness and profundity. Such flowcharts, whenever made, ought to turn out to be a piece of the model's last documentation. There are a few bits of programming that will naturally make model flowcharts; however, most modelers will make them physically utilizing PowerPoint, Visio, or Excel. Of course, almost certainly, your model will be altered during the assembling or as the consequence of an audit. Therefore, if you create the flowchart manually, remember to update it as the design of your model changes.

Practical Exercise: Model Design Customer Support Pricing Model Let's say, for example, that you are offering a customer support option for an existing product. Your financial model needs to answer the question: "How much should we charge per customer per month for support?" You have the following pieces of information:

- You have 500 customers who you think will take up the support offered.
- We expect that each customer will make ten calls per month.
- It is expected to take 5minutes to answer each call and resolve their problem.
- Staff normally answer calls for 6 hours a day, on average, for 20 days per month.
- We are currently paying support center staff $70k per annum.
- There are around $10k in fixed costs per annum.
- We expect to make a 20 percent markup.

Follow these steps to calculate the pricing per customer:
1. Open up a blank Excel file and add a title such as "Customer Support

Pricing Model" in cell B1.

2. Start entering inputs, as shown in Figure 2.8. Enter 500 customers in cell B3 and ten service calls in cell B4 and add the descriptions in column C.

3. Format cells B3 and B4, and all subsequent assumption input cells as inputs using the input style from the Home tab, or your preferred input format. For where to find input styles

4. Calculate the total service calls per month in cell B5 using the formula =B3*B4.

5. In cell B6, enter the average call length of 5 minutes and the description in column C.

6. In B7 cell, ascertain the aggregate of minutes required for all 5,000 service calls using the formula =B5*B6. This now needs to be converted to hours, and this could be done all in one cell, but it's better to lay it out separately so that it's easier to follow.

7. In cell B8, we'll convert the number of minutes to hours using the formula =B7/60. Normally, entering hardcoded numbers into formulas is not considered good practice in financial modeling; however, in this case, we consider that the 60 minutes in an hour is not a variable likely to change, and therefore hardcoding is acceptable.

8. In cell B9, we will also hardcode as the number of available hours is an assumption, but also a formula. Enter the formula =6*20 as we will assume six hours a day, 20 days a month. You could simply enter 120 as a value, but it's better to show how you came up with the number.

9. In cell B10, we then need to figure out how many staff will be required to run the service center. If we need 416 hours per month, and each member of staff has 120 hours available, we can calculate this with the formula =B8/B9. We want to hire full-time staff, so use a ROUNDUP formula to round it up to the nearest decimal place. Your formula should be =ROUNDUP(B8/B9,0).

10. In cell B11, enter the monthly staff costs with the formula=70000/12, bearing in mind that this is also an input cell that might change.

11. The total staff costs can be calculated in cell B12 using the formula =B11*B10.

12. Enter the fixed costs in cell B13 using the formula =10000/12.

13. Add up the total in cell B14 using the formula =B12+B13.

14. Enter the 20 percent markup input in cell B15.

15. Calculate the total revenue in cell B16 using the formula =B14*(1+B15).

16. We can find the unit support price in cell B17 by dividing the total

revenue by the number of customers with the formula =B16/B3.

STEPS TO BUILDING A MODEL

Once the previously mentioned factors have been resolved, you can start to make your model. Most modelers will simply make a plunge and begin building, and while it's acceptable to energize development and innovativeness in making money-related models, it's as yet essential to follow some arranged strides to accomplish the best result. In case you're filling in as the sole money related modeler in an organization or as a specialist, you may have the option to follow a less conventional procedure; thus I've given an increasingly smoothed out form of the means to follow (see "The Streamlined Version," underneath). If you're filling in as a feature of a group of monetary modelers, the means are progressively definite, as it's increasingly imperative to follow an archived and organized procedure, especially if there are numerous modelers and partners giving info (see "The Team Version," further on).

The Streamlined Version, This rendition of the model-building process, is for less conventional ventures, particularly those models intended to be utilized solely by their maker. The seven stages to the smoothed out adaptation are as per the following:

1. Plan the elevated level structure. You're not going to know precisely what the design of the model will be until you delve into it, yet you ought to have some thought of the tabs. Start by gathering the information you have so far into the tabs, as appeared in Figure 2.5.

2. Configuration yields: rundowns, graphs, and reports. Start in view of the end. By pondering the yield of your model at an opportune time simultaneously, you'll be increasingly engaged and will guarantee that every one of your estimations progresses in the direction of the ideal final product.

3. Configuration inputs. Considering the information configuration issues, get your info information into the correct organization or design with the goal that you can connect your figurings to it.

4. Plan figurings by breaking bigger issues into littler ones. Presently begin your calculations. You might start by thinking that all expenses can go on one tab, however on the off chance that staff costs, for instance, start getting

rather convoluted, you may conclude that the staff costs count needs its very own tab.

5. Conclude yields. Connection through your counts to the yields page. Test at each phase to ensure that the model bodes well and change as fundamental.

6. Structure sensitivities and situation investigation. When the model is working accurately, you can include sensitivities and situation examination.

7. Record as you go. Presumptions documentation ought not to be left to the end. Do it as you go!

The Team Version If you are working in a large organization and the modeling project is large, including a few monetary modelers and partners, you'll have to follow an increasingly formal procedure. The bigger the size of the model, and the size of the undertaking, the more forthright task arranging will be required. This itemized procedure is basically to give a structure without one; it ought to in no way, shape or form make the procedure progressively mind-boggling or choke tit, and how intently you adhere to the procedure will rely upon the size and size of the undertaking. The 12 stages have been part of two phases: arranging and building.

Arranging Stage
1. Extension out the undertaking. Survey what should be done so as to finish the model.

■ What is the motivation behind the model? Explain the degree and parameters of the model. Be clear about what the model will be intended to do and its confinements.

■ What is the difficulty we are attempting to explain? Is a model truly required, and is Excel essentially the best arrangement?

■ What's the time span? Make a venture plan by isolating the work that should be done into areas and allocate the assignments and achievements.

2. Dole out venture assignments. When the venture has been characterized and perused, you'll have the option to decide the aptitudes and assets required

to finish the task.

■ What sort of abilities will be required for this undertaking? Ensure you have a parity of industry, money, and business abilities in the group. Consider employing outer advisors if the aptitudes are not accessible in-house.

■ Who will be included? Distinguish the partners who need to give information and approvals on the model. Speak with them about their task necessities and time span desires.

3. Decide the clients of the model. The modeler must realize who will utilize the model, as this will influence the specialized turn of events. Making a model for others to utilize will require structuring an interface that is appropriate for their necessities and, specifically, their degree of nature with Excel. This requires thought of a few issues that sway the model form:

■ Excel form. The modeler needs to consider whether the client might be opening the model in a previous form of Excel. There are a few contemplations the modelers need to make if the model must be perfect with the more established forms of Excel. For instance, the document must be spared as a .xls form, not .xlsx, and the modeler must maintain a strategic distance from a portion of the more current capacities.

■ User amicability. The more vulnerable that clients' aptitudes are with spreadsheets and displaying, the easier to understand the model should be, for instance, by joining more guidelines, control tools(such as drop-down boxes, choice boxes), and straightforward macros. Now and again, a model might be provided to an outsider or made freely accessible, through a site, for instance.

In such cases, the modeler ought to expect the client has an incredibly low degree of Excel ability, and the model ought to be exceptionally secured to ensure that clients don't harm the model.

■ Data approval. The model can be built in order to limit the danger of clients entering mistaken information. For instance, when entering staff names, they may enter "William Jones" as "Will Jones," "W. Jones," "Jones, W.," or some other number of varieties, which can cause mistakes in a model. The modeler must consider how much approval of information sources ought to be incorporated and if mistake messages ought to be given, as this usefulness can be very tedious to construct and test.

■ Frequency of utilization. The modeler needs to consider how yields can be found and created and how frequently the model will be utilized. In the event that the model is to be utilized frequently, the plan of the yields and the time it considers to run should take this. Most models will figure consequently, however increasingly complex models may incorporate a technique that should be physically refreshed or macros that may require some serious energy. In the event that the model is just to be utilized sometimes, it might be of less significance in the event that it takes more time to make the yields each time the model is utilized.

■ Testing and adjusting. Making a model for your own utilization may not require as much work as making a model for other people. Notwithstanding, it is critical to remember that another person should test and approve the model, and others may need to utilize or adjust the model later on. Modelers ought to consistently guarantee that the model is commonly sensible and easy to use.

4. Plan the elevated level structure.

■ The flowchart will incorporate a spot for the info, yields, synopses, and outlines. Prepare a rundown of the considerable yield numbers required and how they might be introduced (e.g., in a table, outline, chart, or another technique). The yields and their introduction organization ought to be considered when planning the format of the model.

■ Translate the flowchart into the model. You ought to have a thought of the number of tabs and how they will be orchestrated inside the model. Attempt to guarantee that the information will stream coherently one way (option to left) all through the model, so connects don't bounce around, making it confounding to the client.

■ Remember to refresh the stream graph if the plan of the model changes during the structure procedure.

5. Make an information assortment plan. Information assortment can be the most tedious piece of a money related displaying venture, so this should be

painstakingly fused into the task intend to guarantee that the information utilized in the model is as precise as could be expected under the circumstances and got on the schedule.

■ Create a rundown of data sources that will be required and where they will be sourced. These will take care of the undertaking plan as assignments.

■ At this stage, you might have the option to recognize information related issues that need consideration and think about answers for foreseen issues. In the event that you are making a hazard register as a feature of the venture arranging process, this is a key hazard. For instance, a few sources of info possibly basic to the model, however, depending on the information being accessible. You should consider chance moderation techniques to guarantee the accessibility and unwavering quality of information to be given by your sources.

■ The model ought to be intended to oblige the configuration in which the fundamental information is accessible, and the yield is required. For instance, if the information is given in a week after week position, however, the yield is required as month to month, you have to consider whether you need to protect the first information as week after week and merge it as a feature of the model, or combine it preceding entering the information into the model.

■ You may even consider planning a data demand structure for sources to fill in with the goal that the information can without much of a stretch be separated and gone into the model. With the arrangement set up and format, structure, and rationale decided, you would now be able to start to fabricate the model.

Building Stage
6. Fabricate inputs.
Enter the information into the info pages. Ensure that you follow best practices by archiving all suppositions and source referencing. It is important this is done as you enter the information, or when you record from where you got the information. In the event that there is any conceivable distortion or absence of lucidity about how figuring functions, ensure that it is expressly reported, either in the computations page or as a major aspect of the suspicions. As information sources become accessible, and the model is

populated with real information, it is important that the wellspring of that information is stayed up with the latest. Source referencing of data sources ought to be adequately nitty-gritty to permit an outsider to follow it back to the source without any problem. Data ought to incorporate title, date, creator, page number, website page, etc., to take into consideration simple following and approval of the model's information. The documentation ought to include:

■ A depiction of the model's usefulness so clients will have the option to see the universally useful of the model and its confinements regularly graphically showed by a stream chart of the model's structure.

■ Instructions on the most proficient way to utilize the model, including a shading code key clarifying the hues and styles utilized in the model.

■ If a count or information point in one area is dealt with uniquely in contrast to the remainder of the model, a clarification of the explanation behind the distinction.

■ Changes to the structure of a model in the variant sign on the spread page, itemizing what auxiliary or significant changes were done, when, and by whom.

7. Assemble estimations and activities.
Building exact and obviously auditable computations is a basic advance in building a monetary model. An intelligent figuring ought to permit clients to follow and follow the computation effectively—from the contributions to the yields, and back once more.

■ Follow best practices by connecting to include cells, just enter information once, and consistently allude to the first source's cell where conceivable, instead of connecting to another connection.

■ Don't blend hardcoded information in with recipes. On the off chance that you've to hard code a number into a cell, it ought to be remembered for the suspicions or source datasheet and connected from that point.

■ Try to work from left to right and start to finish where conceivable.

■ Use name goes in Excel to name single-cell constants or tables of data sources. This can make it simpler to assemble and approve recipes in a money related model.

■ Use the unrivaled technique and the most proficient capacities. This strategy will be the least complex, generally proficient, and most straightforward to follow.

■Link coherently all through the model. Attempt to ensure joins go one way (from left to right) rather than hopping in reverse and advances between various tabs.

■ Build blunder checks at every possible opportunity, and sense check and test for mistakes as you go.

■ Double-check estimations are utilizing elective figuring techniques or by physically computing from first standards.

■ Document the estimations and their rationale as you go; don't leave everything as far as possible. Your procedure may appear glaringly evident to you at that point; however, it is presumably not satisfactory to another person checking on your model. There is a genuinely high probability that, later on, you won't recollect why you've determined something a specific way.

■ Long counts ought to be separated into intelligent parts of more straightforward computations. This will stay away from one long recipe in Excel, making it more obvious, test, and update, and enormously decrease the chance of mistake.

■ A progressively definite flowchart growing out the estimations into subcomponents might be the clearest approach to introduce the model's rationale if a computation is especially intricate. This should be possible in Excel by taking a model bit of information and recording its stream all through the computations.

8. Construct yields: outlines, graphs, and reports. Start to sum up the count on the yield page.

■ Continue to test and check for equations and rationale blunders at each phase of the building.

■ Follow best practices as sketched out above for yields just as estimations.

9. Friend and customer survey of the draft model.
Presently that the model's plan, rationale, and estimations have been resolved, it is essential to experience it with the remainder of the group to guarantee that the model meets its motivation. Get the group together, take key info, and finish it from start to finish. The planning of this survey is significant, as it needs to happen after a portion of the model has been worked, to permit the analysts to check the normal yields and how the model works practically speaking; in any case, the model ought not to be finished at this point on the off chance that there are huge basic changes required because of the audit. Not exclusively should a model tackle the issue for which it is planned; client acknowledgment of the model is additionally significant. Customers (end clients) must acknowledge and comprehend the model. A walkthrough at this stage may help to distinguish territories where remedies or adjustments are required and will likewise permit the client to get comfortable with how the model is proposed to function. Components to be considered in the companion draft audit are:

■ Walkthrough the estimations: Are they exact at an elevated level?

■ Are the presumptions and source information unmistakably driving the yield?

■ Does the model take care of the difficulty it is being intended to settle?

■ Are the stream and structure simple to follow? Note that this companion survey is your last opportunity to guarantee that there are no recipe or rationale mistakes in the model before the proper quality confirmation (QA) of the model. Modelers ought to be sure that their models submitted for formal QA are liberated from botches.

10. Plan sensitivities and situation examination.
When the base model is finished and working accurately, you can include sensitivities and situation investigation. The contributions for situation examination might not have been resolved as a component of the arranging procedure, and since the base model is finished, you will have the option to

test the contributions to see their effect. This may impact your choice with regards to what to appear in the situation investigation.

11. Formal model QA check.

This last QA check of the model is a conventional procedure and ought not to be mistaken for the consistent testing and troubleshooting that ought to have occurred during the model form. It is the modeler's duty to guarantee that the model is exact, hearty, and operational. The QA procedure ought not to reveal equation or rationale blunders at this late stage, and the discovery of such will raise questions about the competency of the modeler. The model's last QA testing process incorporates:

■ Stress testing the contributions with a wide scope of qualities to check the internal activities of the model.

This incorporates testing esteems at the boundaries to guarantee that the model procedures the contribution true to form, particularly where approval and insurance are utilized. Additionally, test a wide range and blend of information factors, as some concealed bugs may exist in the estimations. Utilizing 0 or 1 can assist with featuring clear mistakes, as the yields ought to be basic. For instance, a unit cost of zero ought to produce an income of zero, and on the off chance that it does not, you'll have to research why not.

■ Check that Excel mistakes such as "#DIV/0!" have not been activated by entering zeros or other invalid information as data sources.

■ Make sure that all data sources can, in any case, be entered appropriately. By applying insurance to a model, a modeler can unintentionally cause switches and drop-downs to quit working. On the off chance that insurance is applied, extra testing and looking voluntarily should be conveyed.

■ Check the affectability of yields (subordinate factors) to changes in the information sources (autonomous factors). Some portion of the QA procedure ought to be to watch that the heading and extent of the change are as per how you consistently anticipate that the yields should act.

■ Check all documentation for spelling, language structure, shading coding consistency, and introduction.

■ As the model experiences a few cycles, it's entirely expected to locate that excess counts are incorporated despite the fact that they are not, at this point, helpful or relevant to the model. Following wards is helpful for recognizing input information that isn't being utilized.

12. Keep up the model.
When a model is finished and given to the clients, all things considered, eventually—weeks, months, or years after the model has been finished—support or refreshing of the model should be attempted. On the off chance that it's essential to change inputs, this should be possible by the client, however on the off chance that the change is major or basic, a model engineer ought to be the one to roll out the improvements. Contingent upon the accessibility of assets, it is ideal that an individual from the first model-building group attempt the update, however on the off chance that accepted procedures have been followed all through the manufacturing procedure, in the event that it has been very much recorded and worked in a hearty manner, and if the modeler doing the update is knowledgeable in monetary displaying method, refreshing the model ought not to represent any issue. At the point where the model is refreshed or revised, particularly if the change is auxiliary, rendition control forms should be followed to guarantee that the right form of the model is utilized. The following is some more data on the best way to record forms accurately.

DELVE INTO KEY FINANCIAL, STATISTICAL, AND TIME FUNCTIONS

Notwithstanding recipes, another approach to lead numerical calculations in Excel is through capacities. Factual capacities apply a scientific procedure to a gathering of cells in a worksheet. For instance, the SUM work is utilized to include the qualities contained in a scope of cells. A rundown of regularly utilized measurable capacities appears in Table 2.4. Capacities are more proficient than equations when you are applying a scientific procedure to a gathering of cells. On the off chance that you make use of an equation to include the qualities in a scope of cells, you would need to add every cell area to the recipe each in turn. This can be very tedious in the event that you need to include the qualities in a couple of hundred cell areas. In any case, when you utilize a capacity, you can feature all the cells that contain values you wish to the whole in only one stage. This segment shows an assortment of measurable capacities that we will add to the Personal Budget exercise manual. Notwithstanding showing capacities, this segment likewise surveys percent of complete counts and the utilization of supreme references.

Table 2.4 Commonly Used Statistical Functions

Statistical Functions	Output
ABS	The total estimation of a number
AVERAGE	The normal or math mean for a gathering of numbers.
COUNT	The number of cell areas in a range that contain a numeric character
COUNTA	The number of cell areas in a range that contain a book or numeric character
MAX	The most noteworthy numeric incentive in a gathering of numbers

MIDDLE	The center number in a gathering of numbers (a large portion of the numbers in the gathering are higher than the middle, and a large portion of the numbers in the gathering are lower than the middle)
MIN	The most reduced numeric incentive in a gathering of numbers
MODE	The number that shows up most regularly in a gathering of numbers
PRODUCT	The consequence of duplicating all the qualities in a scope of cell areas
SQRT	The positive square base of a number
STDEV.S	The standard deviation for a gathering of numbers dependent on an example
SUM	The aggregate of every single numeric incentive in a gathering

The SUM Function

The SUM work is utilized when you have to figure sums for a scope of cells or a gathering of chosen cells on a worksheet. With respect to the Budget Detail worksheet, we will utilize the SUM capacity to figure the aggregates in line 12. It is critical to take note that there are a few techniques for adding capacity to a worksheet, which will be exhibited all through the rest of this section. The accompanying shows how capacity can be added to a worksheet by composing it into a cell area:

Snap the Budget Detail worksheet tab to open the worksheet.

Snap cell C12.

Type an equivalent sign =.

Type the capacity name SUM.

Type an open enclosure (.

Snap cell C3 and drag down to cell C11. This places the range C3: C11 into the capacity.

Type an end enclosure).

Press the ENTER key. The capacity ascertains the aggregate for the Monthly Spend section, which is $1,496.

The figure below shows the presence of the SUM work added to the Budget Detail worksheet before squeezing the ENTER key.

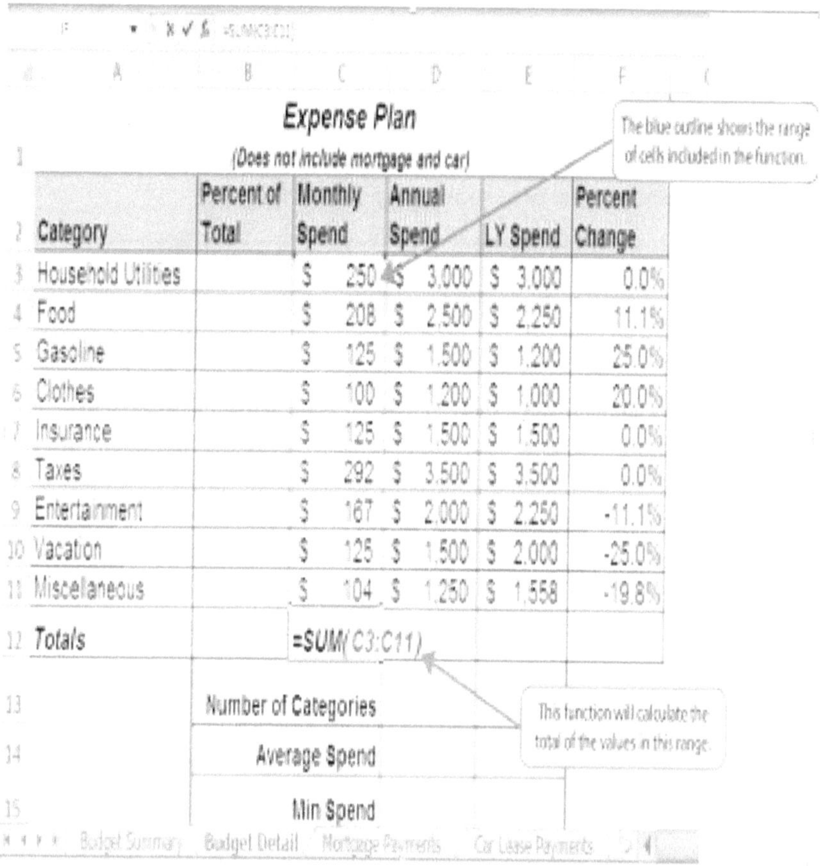

	A	B	C	D	E	F	
				X ✓ ƒx =SUM(C3:C11)			

Expense Plan

(Does not include mortgage and car)

Category	Percent of Total	Monthly Spend	Annual Spend	LY Spend	Percent Change
Household Utilities		$ 250	$ 3,000	$ 3,000	0.0%
Food		$ 208	$ 2,500	$ 2,250	11.1%
Gasoline		$ 125	$ 1,500	$ 1,200	25.0%
Clothes		$ 100	$ 1,200	$ 1,000	20.0%
Insurance		$ 125	$ 1,500	$ 1,500	0.0%
Taxes		$ 292	$ 3,500	$ 3,500	0.0%
Entertainment		$ 167	$ 2,000	$ 2,250	-11.1%
Vacation		$ 125	$ 1,500	$ 2,000	-25.0%
Miscellaneous		$ 104	$ 1,250	$ 1,558	-19.8%
Totals		=SUM(C3:C11)			
	Number of Categories				
	Average Spend				
	Min Spend				

Including the SUM Function to the Budget Detail Worksheet

As appeared in the figure above, the SUM work was added to cell C12. In any case, this capacity is additionally expected to ascertain the aggregates in the Annual Spend and LY Spend sections. The capacity can be reordered into these cell areas on account of relative referencing. Relative referencing fills an indistinguishable need for capacities from it accomplishes for recipes. The accompanying exhibits how the absolute line is finished:

Snap cell C12 in the Budget Detail worksheet.

Snap the Copy button in the Home tab of the Ribbon.

Feature cells D12 and E12.

Snap the Paste button in the Home tab of the Ribbon. This glues the SUM work into cells D12 and E12 and computes the sums for these sections.

Snap cell F11.

Snap the Copy button in the Home tab of the Ribbon.

Snap cell F12, at that point, click the Paste button in the Home tab of the Ribbon. Since we presently have sums in column 12, we can glue the percent change recipe into this line.

Figure 2 shows the yield of the SUM work that was added to cells C12, D12, and E12. What's more, the percent change recipe was reordered into cell F12. Notice that this form of the financial plan is arranging a 1.7% lessening in spending contrasted with a year ago.

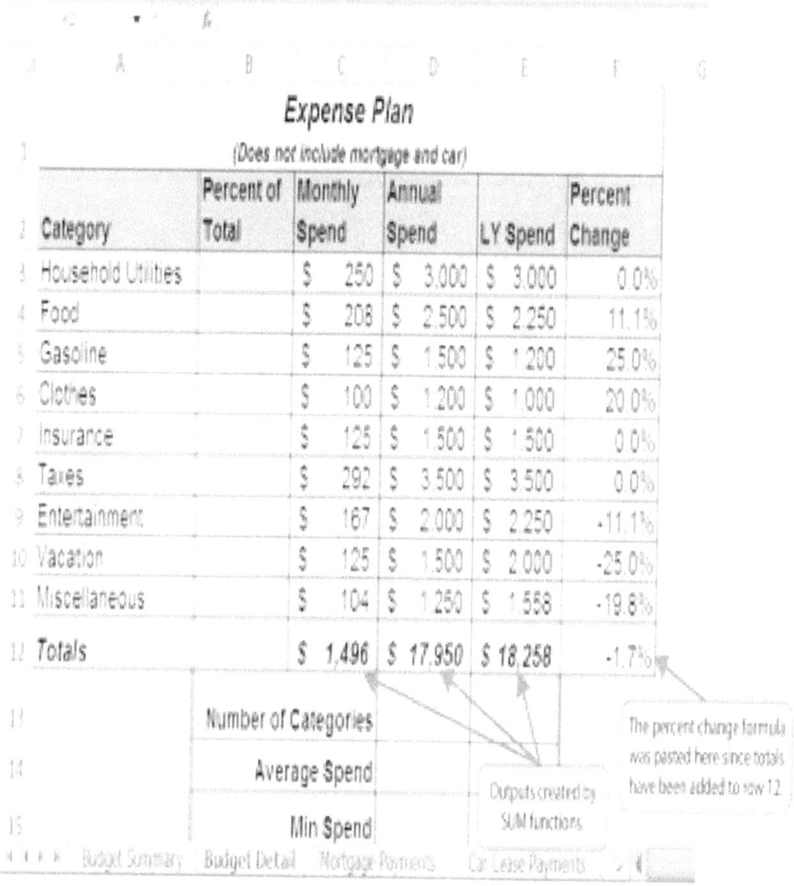

	A	B	C	D	E	F
1		Expense Plan (Does not include mortgage and car)				
2	Category	Percent of Total	Monthly Spend	Annual Spend	LY Spend	Percent Change
3	Household Utilities		$ 250	$ 3,000	$ 3,000	0.0%
4	Food		$ 208	$ 2,500	$ 2,250	11.1%
5	Gasoline		$ 125	$ 1,500	$ 1,200	25.0%
6	Clothes		$ 100	$ 1,200	$ 1,000	20.0%
7	Insurance		$ 125	$ 1,500	$ 1,500	0.0%
8	Taxes		$ 292	$ 3,500	$ 3,500	0.0%
9	Entertainment		$ 167	$ 2,000	$ 2,250	-11.1%
10	Vacation		$ 125	$ 1,500	$ 2,000	-25.0%
11	Miscellaneous		$ 104	$ 1,250	$ 1,558	-19.8%
12	Totals		$ 1,496	$ 17,950	$ 18,258	-1.7%
13		Number of Categories				
14		Average Spend				
15		Min Spend				

Figure 2: Results of the Function, SUM in the Budget Detail Worksheet

Respectability Check
Cell Ranges in Statistical Functions

At the point when you expect to utilize a factual capacity on a scope of cells in a worksheet, ensure there are two cell areas isolated by a colon and not a comma. In the event that you enter two cell areas isolated by a comma, the capacity will deliver a yield; however, it will be applied to just two cell areas rather than a scope of cells. For instance, the SUM work that appeared in Figure 3 will include just the qualities in cell C3 and cell C11, not the range C3: C11.

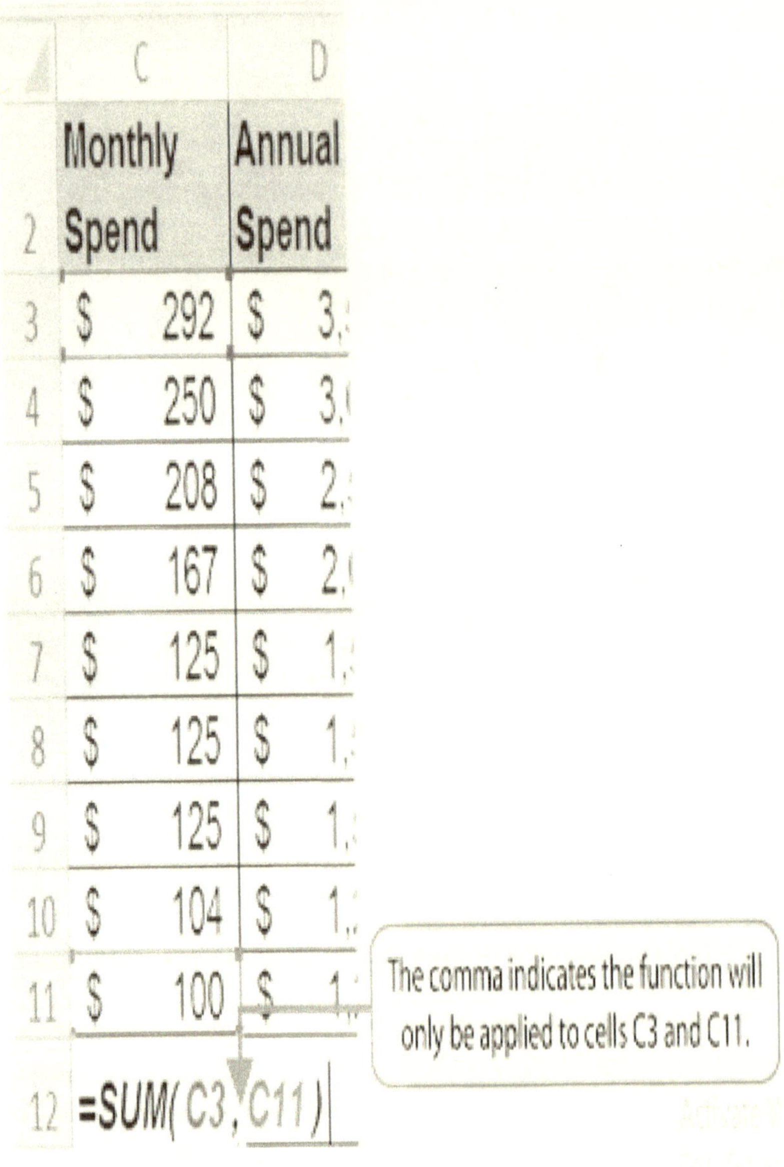

Figure 3: SUM Function Adding Two Cell Locations

Supreme References (Calculating Percent of Totals)

Information record: Continue with CH2 Personal Budget.
Since sums were added to push 12 of the Budget Detail worksheet, a percent of all-out figuring can be added to Column B starting in cell B3. The percent of all-out count shows the rate for each an incentive in the Annual Spend segment concerning the aggregate in cell D12. Be that as it may, after the recipe is made, it will be important to kill Excel's relative referencing highlight before reordering the equation to the remainder of the phone areas in the segment. Killing Excel's relative referencing highlight is practiced through a flat out reference. The accompanying advances clarify how this is finished:

Snap cell B3 in the Budget Detail worksheet.

Type an equivalent sign =.

Snap cell D3.

Type a forward slice/.

Snap cell D12.

Press the ENTER key. You will see that Household Utilities speaks to 16.7% of the Annual Spend financial plan (see Figure 4).

B3 f_x =D3/D12

Expense Plan

(Does not include mortgage and car)

Category	Percent of Total	Monthly Spend	Annual Spend	LY Spend	Percent Change
Household Utilities	16.7%	$ 250	$ 3,000	$ 3,000	0.0%
Food		$ 208	$ 2,500	$ 2,250	11.1%
Gasoline		$ 125	$ 1,500	$ 1,200	25.0%
Clothes		$ 100	$ 1,200	$ 1,000	20.0%
Insurance		$ 125	$ 1,500	$ 1,500	0.0%
Taxes		$ 292	$ 3,500	$ 3,500	0.0%
Entertainment		$ 167	$ 2,000	$ 2,250	-11.1%
Vacation		$ 125	$ 1,500	$ 2,000	-25.0%
Miscellaneous		$ 104	$ 1,250	$ 1,558	-19.8%
Totals		$ 1,496	$ 17,950	$ 18,258	-1.7%

Number of Categories

Average Spend

Min Spend

Figure 4: Adding a Formula to Calculate the Percent of Total

Figure 4 shows the finished recipe that is computing the rate that Household Utilities Annual Spend speaks to the all-out Annual Spend for the financial plan (see cell B3). Ordinarily, we would duplicate this recipe and glue it into the range B4: B11. Irrespective, due to relative referencing, both cell references will increment by one column as the recipe is stuck into the cells underneath B3. This is fine for the principal cell reference in the recipe (D3);

however, not for the subsequent cell reference (D12). Figure 2.15 outlines what occurs in the event that we glue the recipe into the range B4: B12 in its present state. Notice that Excel produces the #DIV/0 mistake code. This implies Excel is attempting to separate a number by zero, which is incomprehensible. Taking a gander at the recipe in cell B4, you see that the primary cell reference was changed from D3 to D4. This is fine since we currently need to separate the Annual Spend for Insurance by the complete Annual Spend in cell D12. Nonetheless, Excel has additionally changed the D12 cell reference to D13. Since cell area D13 is clear, the recipe creates the #DIV/0 blunder code.

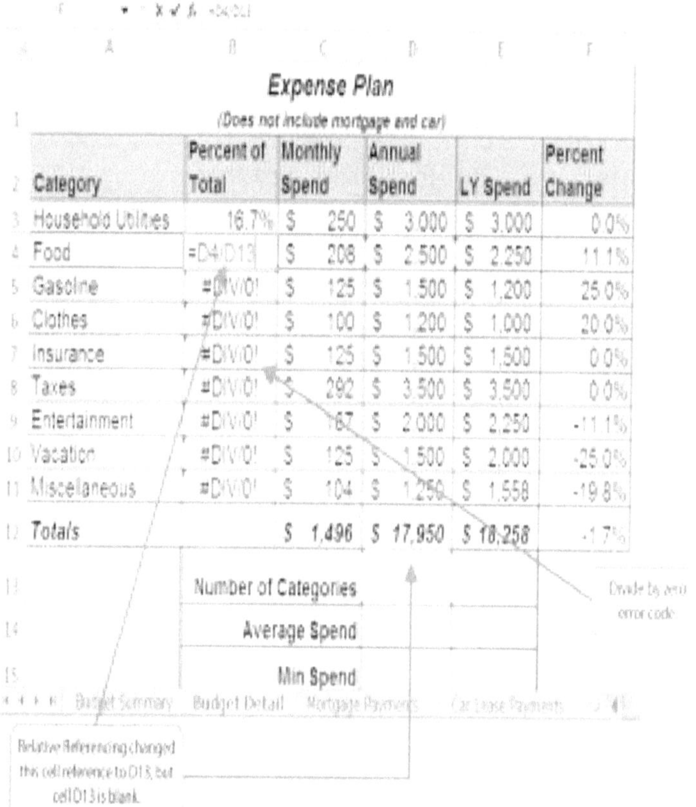

Expense Plan

(Does not include mortgage and car)

Category	Percent of Total	Monthly Spend	Annual Spend	LY Spend	Percent Change
Household Utilities	16.7%	$ 250	$ 3,000	$ 3,000	0.0%
Food	=D4/D13	$ 208	$ 2,500	$ 2,250	11.1%
Gasoline	#DIV/0!	$ 125	$ 1,500	$ 1,200	25.0%
Clothes	#DIV/0!	$ 100	$ 1,200	$ 1,000	20.0%
Insurance	#DIV/0!	$ 125	$ 1,500	$ 1,500	0.0%
Taxes	#DIV/0!	$ 292	$ 3,500	$ 3,500	0.0%
Entertainment	#DIV/0!	$ 167	$ 2,000	$ 2,250	-11.1%
Vacation	#DIV/0!	$ 125	$ 1,500	$ 2,000	-25.0%
Miscellaneous	#DIV/0!	$ 104	$ 1,250	$ 1,558	-19.8%
Totals		$ 1,496	$ 17,950	$ 18,258	-1.7%
Number of Categories					
Average Spend					
Min Spend					

Figure 5 #DIV/0 Error from Relative Referencing

To wipe out the gap by-zero mistake that appeared in Figure 5, we should add an outright reference to cell D12 in the equation. An outright reference forestalls relative referencing from changing a cell reference in a recipe. This is likewise alluded to as locking a cell. The accompanying clarifies how this is cultivated:

Double-tap cell B3.

Spot the mouse pointer before D12 and snap. The squinting cursor ought to be before the D in the cell reference D12.

Press the F4 key. You will see a dollar sign ($) included in front of the section letter D and line number 12. You can likewise type the dollar signs before the segment letter and line number.

Press the ENTER key.
Snap cell B3.
Snap the Copy button in the Home tab of the Ribbon.
Feature the range B4: B11.
Snap the Paste button in the Home tab of the Ribbon.

Figure 6 shows the percent of all-out equation with a flat out reference added to D12. Take note that in cell B4, the reference of the cell remains D12 as opposed to changing to D13, as appeared in Figure 5. Likewise, you will see that the rates are being determined in the remainder of the cells in the segment, and the partition by-zero blunder is currently killed.

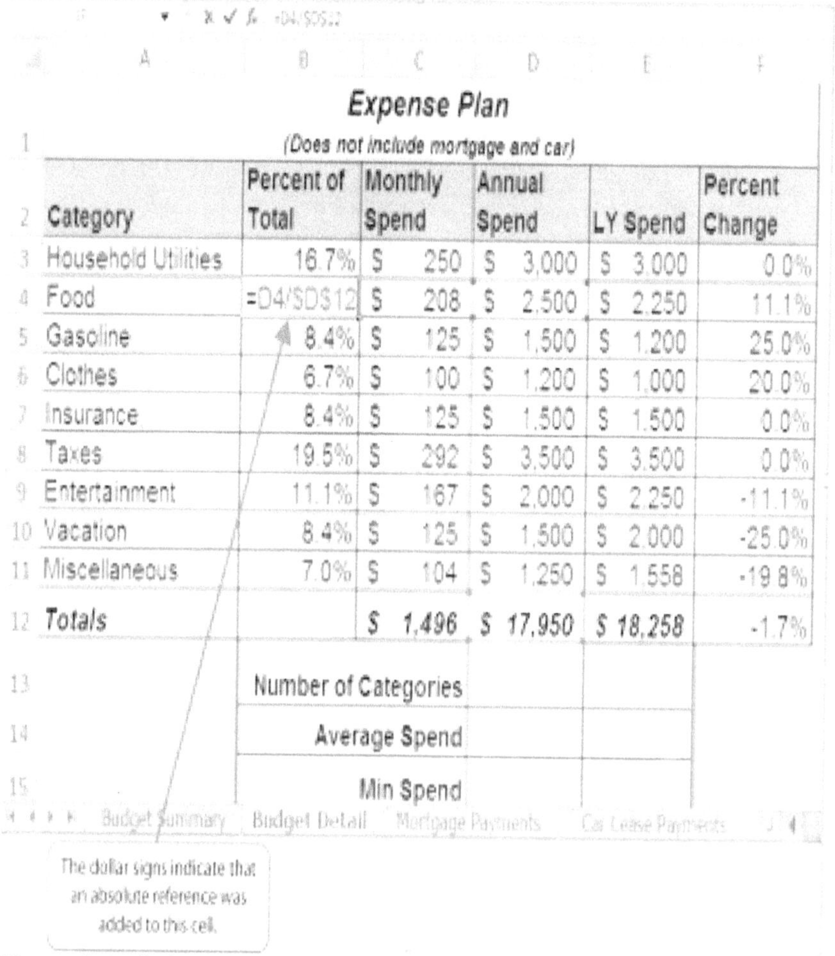

f = =D4/$D$12

	A	B	C	D	E	F

Expense Plan
(Does not include mortgage and car)

Category	Percent of Total	Monthly Spend	Annual Spend	LY Spend	Percent Change
Household Utilities	16.7%	$ 250	$ 3,000	$ 3.000	0.0%
Food	=D4/$D$12	$ 208	$ 2.500	$ 2.250	11.1%
Gasoline	8.4%	$ 125	$ 1,500	$ 1.200	25.0%
Clothes	6.7%	$ 100	$ 1,200	$ 1.000	20.0%
Insurance	8.4%	$ 125	$ 1,500	$ 1.500	0.0%
Taxes	19.5%	$ 292	$ 3,500	$ 3.500	0.0%
Entertainment	11.1%	$ 167	$ 2.000	$ 2.250	-11.1%
Vacation	8.4%	$ 125	$ 1.500	$ 2.000	-25.0%
Miscellaneous	7.0%	$ 104	$ 1.250	$ 1.558	-19.8%
Totals		$ 1,496	$ 17,950	$ 18,258	-1.7%
Number of Categories					
Average Spend					
Min Spend					

Figure 6: Including an Absolute Reference to a Cell Reference in a Formula

Ability Refresher
Total References

Snap before the segment letter of a cell reference in a recipe or capacity that you don't need to be changed when the equation or capacity is stuck into another cell area.

Hit the F4 key or type a dollar sign $ before the section letter and line number of the cell reference.

The COUNT Function

Information record: Continue with CH2 Personal Budget.
The following capacity that we will add to the Budget Detail worksheet is the COUNT work. The COUNT work is utilized to decide what number of cells in a range contain a numeric section. The COUNT capacity won't work for checking content or other non-numeric sections. For the Budget Detail worksheet, we will utilize the COUNT capacity to tally the number of things that are arranged in the Annual Spend section (Column D). The accompanying clarifies how the COUNT work is added to the worksheet by utilizing the capacity list:

Snap cell D13 in the Budget Detail worksheet.
Type an equivalent sign =.
Type the letter C.

Snap the down bolt on the parchment bar of the capacity list (see Figure 2.17) and discover the word COUNT.

Double-tap the word COUNT from the capacity list.
Feature the range D3: D11.

You can type an end bracket) and afterward press the ENTER key, or essentially press the ENTER key, and Excel will close the capacity for you. The capacity delivers a yield of 9 since there are nine things anticipated in the worksheet.
Figure 7 shows the capacity list box that shows up in the wake of finishing stages 2 and 3 for the COUNT work. The capacity list gives an elective strategy to add capacity to a worksheet.

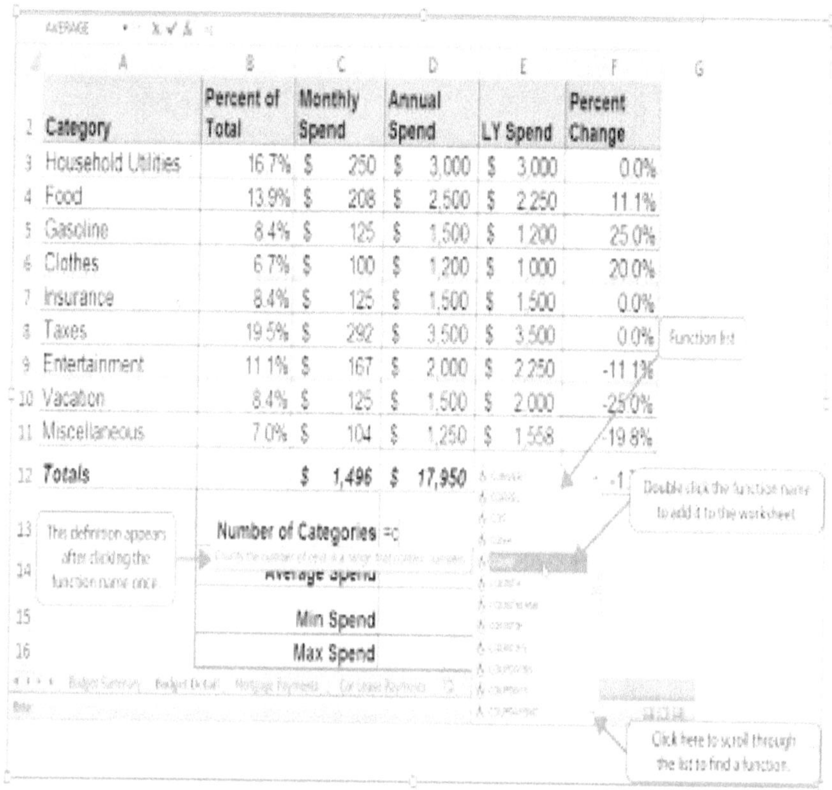

Figure 7 Using the Function List to Add the COUNT Function

Figure 8 shows the yield of the COUNT work subsequent to squeezing the ENTER key. The capacity includes the number of cells in the range D3: D11 that contains a numeric worth. The aftereffect of 9 demonstrates that there are nine classifications anticipated in this spending plan.

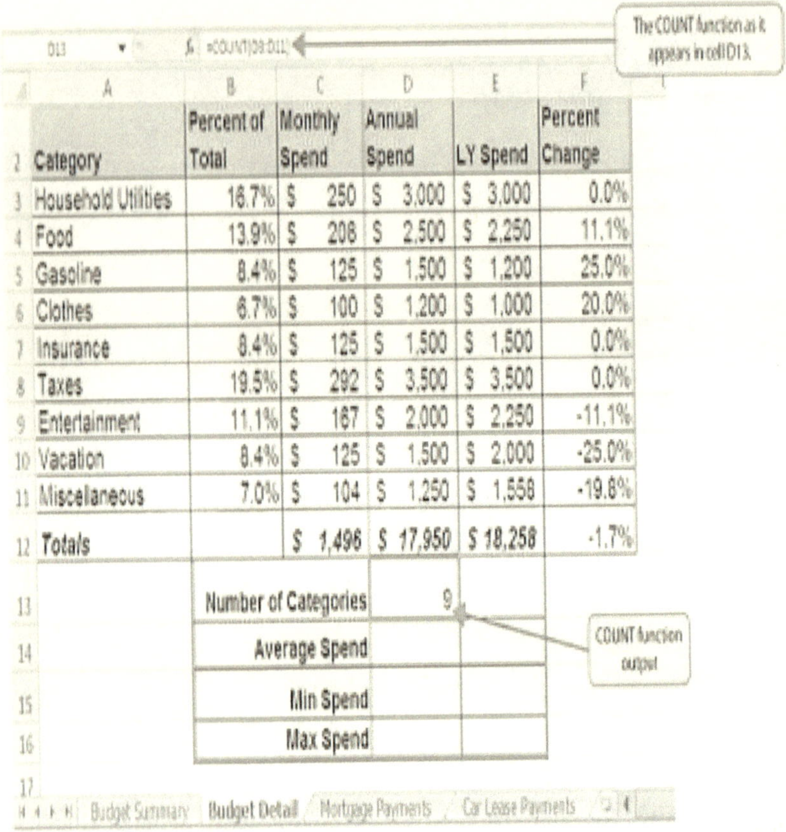

Category	Percent of Total	Monthly Spend	Annual Spend	LY Spend	Percent Change
Household Utilities	16.7%	$ 250	$ 3,000	$ 3,000	0.0%
Food	13.9%	$ 208	$ 2,500	$ 2,250	11.1%
Gasoline	8.4%	$ 125	$ 1,500	$ 1,200	25.0%
Clothes	6.7%	$ 100	$ 1,200	$ 1,000	20.0%
Insurance	8.4%	$ 125	$ 1,500	$ 1,500	0.0%
Taxes	19.5%	$ 292	$ 3,500	$ 3,500	0.0%
Entertainment	11.1%	$ 167	$ 2,000	$ 2,250	-11.1%
Vacation	8.4%	$ 125	$ 1,500	$ 2,000	-25.0%
Miscellaneous	7.0%	$ 104	$ 1,250	$ 1,558	-19.8%
Totals		$ 1,496	$ 17,950	$ 18,258	-1.7%
Number of Categories		9			
Average Spend					
Min Spend					
Max Spend					

Budget Summary | Budget Detail | Mortgage Payments | Car Lease Payments

Figure 8 Completed COUNT Function in the Budget Detail Worksheet

The AVERAGE Function

The following capacity we will add to the Budget Detail worksheet is the AVERAGE capacity. This capacity is utilized to compute the number-crunching mean for a gathering of numbers. For the Budget Detail worksheet, we will utilize the capacity to ascertain the normal of the qualities in the Annual Spend segment. We would add this to the worksheet by utilizing the Function Library. The accompanying advances clarify how this is cultivated:

Snap cell D14 in the Budget Detail worksheet.
Snap the Formulas tab on the Ribbon.
Snap the More Functions button in the Function Library gathering of orders.
Spot the mouse pointer over the Statistical alternative starting from the drop rundown of choices.

Snap the AVERAGE capacity name from the rundown of capacities that show up in the menu (see Figure 9). This opens the Function Arguments exchange box.

Snap the Collapse Dialog button in the Function Arguments exchange box (see Figure 2.20).

Feature the range D3: D11.

Snap the Expand Dialog button in the Function Arguments discourse box (see Figure 2.21). You can likewise press the ENTER key to get a similar outcome.

Snap the OK button on the Function Arguments exchange box. This adds the AVERAGE capacity to the worksheet.

Figure 9 shows how capacity is chosen from the Function Library in the Formulas tab of the Ribbon.

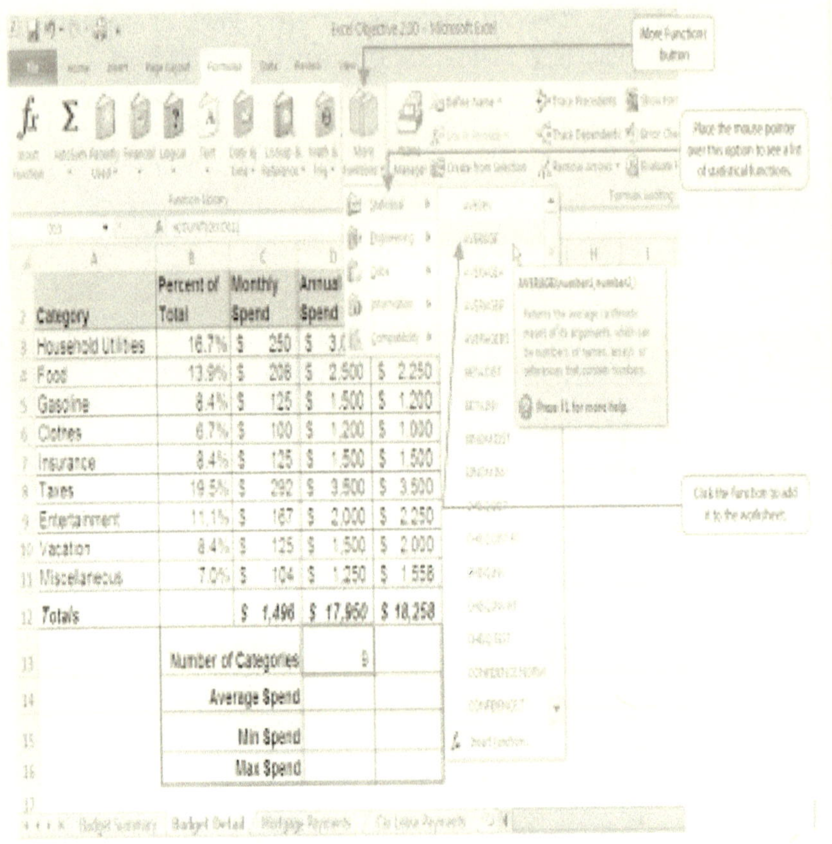

Figure 9 Selecting the AVERAGE Function from the Function Library

Figure 10 shows the Function Arguments discourse box. This shows up after capacity is chosen from the Function Library. The Collapse Dialog button is utilized to shroud the discourse box so a scope of cells can be featured on the worksheet and afterward added to the capacity.

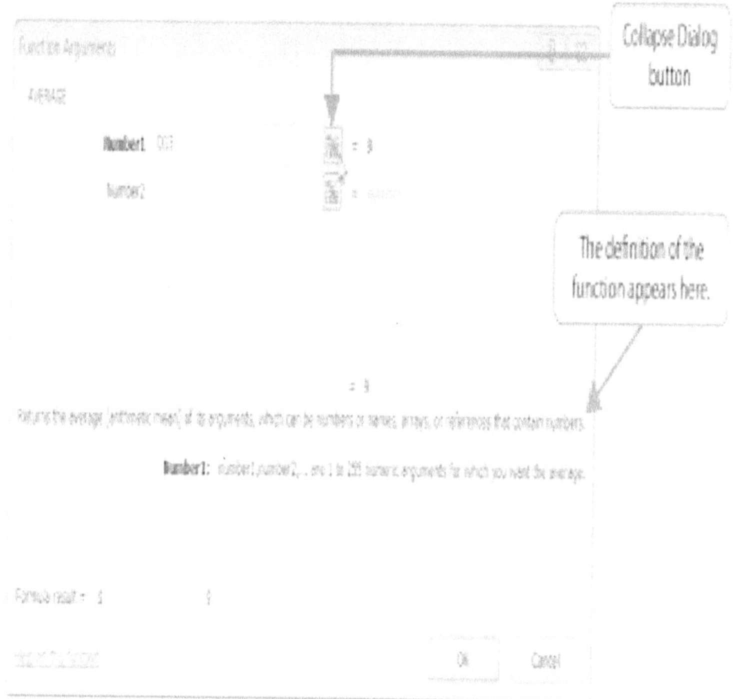

Figure 10 Function Arguments Dialog Box

Figure 11 shows how a scope of cells can be chosen from the Function Arguments discourse box once it has been fell.

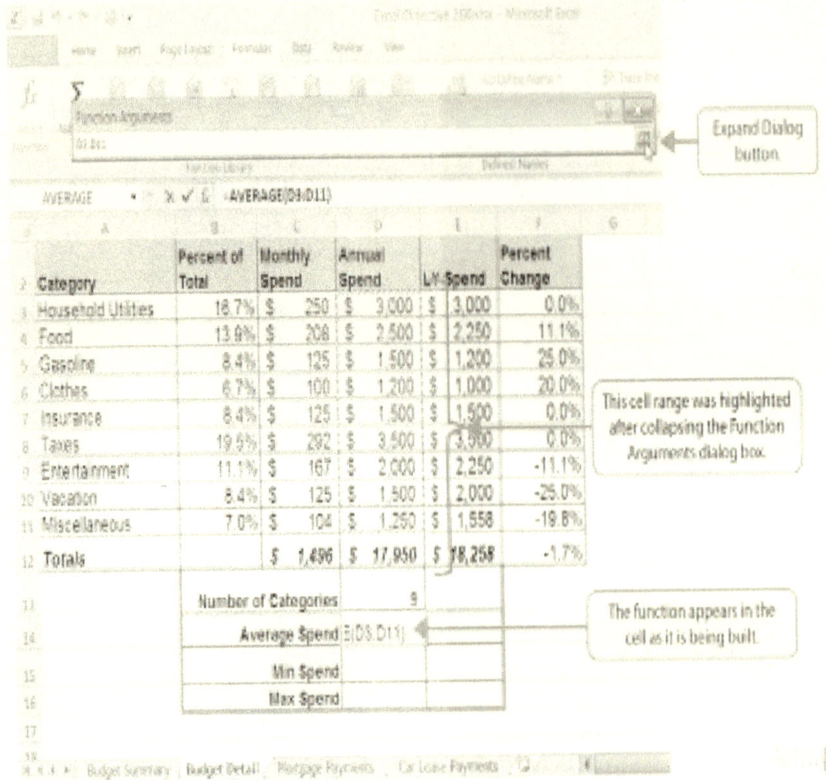

Figure 11 Selecting a Range from the Function Arguments Dialog Box

Figure 12 shows the Function Arguments exchange box after the cell extends is characterized by the AVERAGE capacity. The discourse box shows the aftereffect of the capacity before it is added to the cell area. This permits you to survey the capacity yield to decide if it bodes well before adding it to the worksheet.

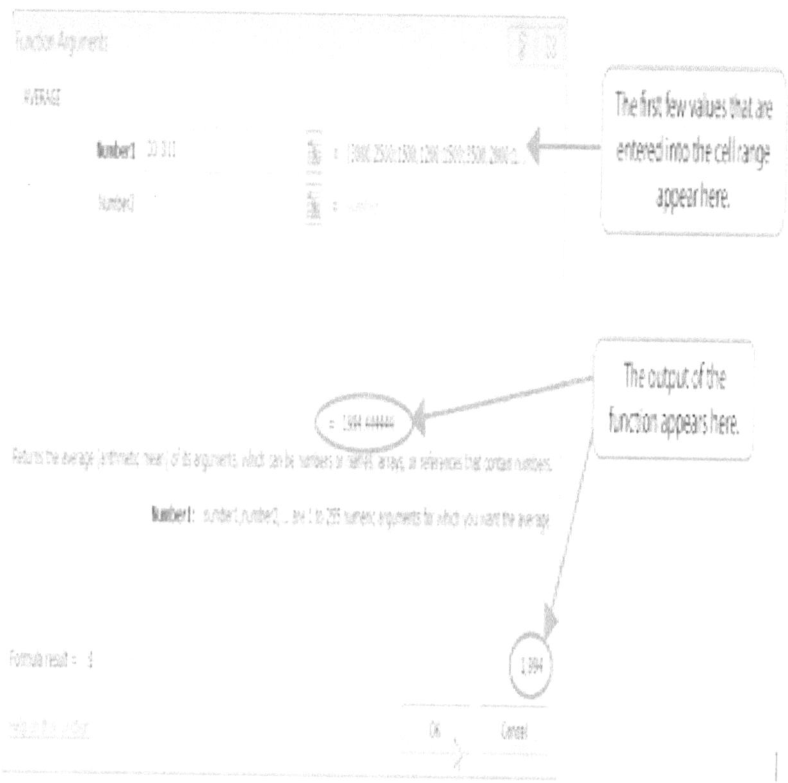

Figure 12 Function Arguments Dialog Box after a Cell Range Is Defined for a Function

Figure 13 shows the finished AVERAGE capacity in the Budget Detail worksheet. The yield of the capacity shows that on normal, we hope to burn through $1,994 for every one of the classes recorded in Column An of the spending plan. This normal spend figuring per class can be utilized as a pointer to figure out which classifications are costing pretty much than the normally planned spend dollars.

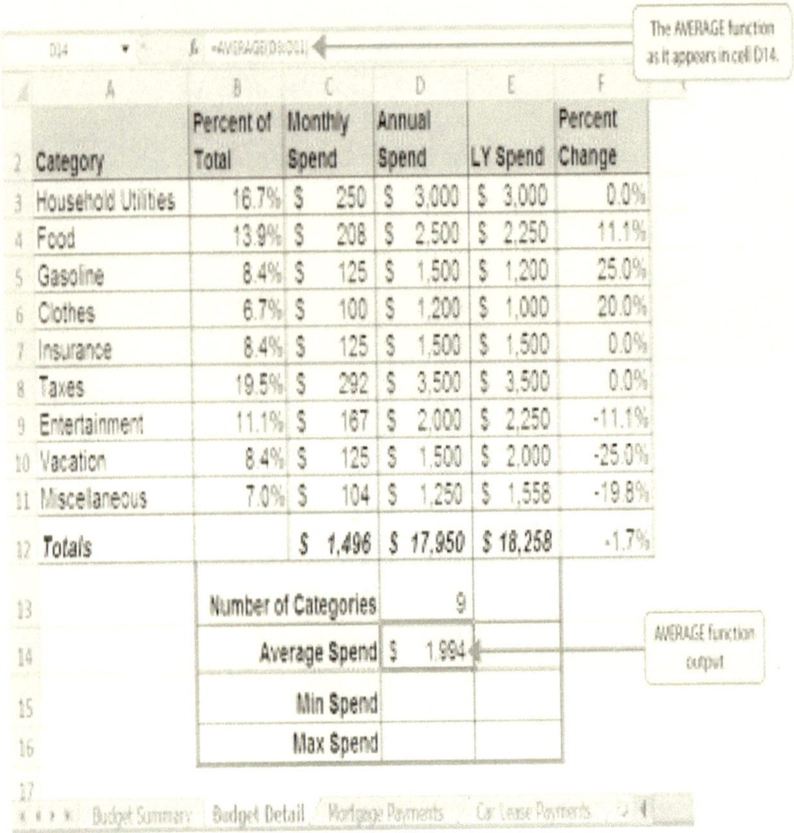

The AVERAGE function as it appears in cell D14.

Category	Percent of Total	Monthly Spend	Annual Spend	LY Spend	Percent Change
Household Utilities	16.7%	$ 250	$ 3,000	$ 3,000	0.0%
Food	13.9%	$ 208	$ 2,500	$ 2,250	11.1%
Gasoline	8.4%	$ 125	$ 1,500	$ 1,200	25.0%
Clothes	6.7%	$ 100	$ 1,200	$ 1,000	20.0%
Insurance	8.4%	$ 125	$ 1,500	$ 1,500	0.0%
Taxes	19.5%	$ 292	$ 3,500	$ 3,500	0.0%
Entertainment	11.1%	$ 167	$ 2,000	$ 2,250	-11.1%
Vacation	8.4%	$ 125	$ 1,500	$ 2,000	-25.0%
Miscellaneous	7.0%	$ 104	$ 1,250	$ 1,558	-19.8%
Totals		$ 1,496	$ 17,950	$ 18,258	-1.7%
	Number of Categories		9		
	Average Spend	$ 1,994			
	Min Spend				
	Max Spend				

AVERAGE function output

Budget Summary   Budget Detail   Mortgage Payments   Car Lease Payments

Figure 13 Completed AVERAGE Function

The MAX and MIN Functions

Information document: Continue with CH2 Personal Budget.
The last two measurable capacities that we will add to the Budget Detail worksheet are the MAX and MIN capacities. These capacities distinguish the most noteworthy and least qualities in the scope of cells. The accompanying advances disclose how to add these capacities to the Budget Detail worksheet:

Snap cell D15 in the Budget Detail worksheet.

Type an equivalent sign =.
Type the word MIN.

Type an open bracket (.
Feature the range D3: D11.

Type an end bracket) and press the ENTER key, or essentially press the ENTER key, and Excel will close the capacity for you. The MIN work delivers a yield of $1,200, which is the most minimal incentive in the Annual Spend segment (see Figure 14).

Snap cell D16.
Type an equivalent sign =.
Type the word MAX.
Type an open bracket (.
Feature the range D3: D11.

Type an end bracket) and press the ENTER key, or essentially press the ENTER key, and Excel will close the capacity for you. The MAX work delivers a yield of $3,500. This is the most noteworthy incentive in the Annual Spend section (see Figure 15).

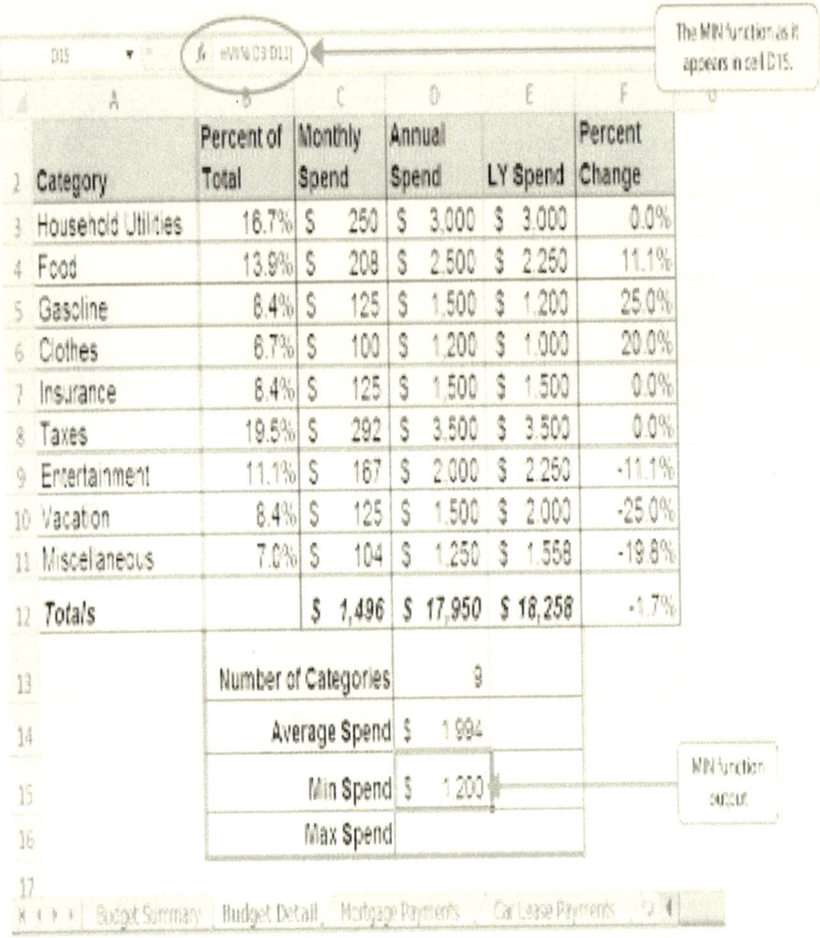

	A		B	C	D	E	F	
	Category		Percent of Total	Monthly Spend	Annual Spend	LY Spend	Percent Change	
3	Household Utilities		16.7%	$ 250	$ 3,000	$ 3,000	0.0%	
4	Food		13.9%	$ 208	$ 2,500	$ 2,250	11.1%	
5	Gasoline		8.4%	$ 125	$ 1,500	$ 1,200	25.0%	
6	Clothes		6.7%	$ 100	$ 1,200	$ 1,000	20.0%	
7	Insurance		8.4%	$ 125	$ 1,500	$ 1,500	0.0%	
8	Taxes		19.5%	$ 292	$ 3,500	$ 3,500	0.0%	
9	Entertainment		11.1%	$ 167	$ 2,000	$ 2,250	-11.1%	
10	Vacation		8.4%	$ 125	$ 1,500	$ 2,000	-25.0%	
11	Miscellaneous		7.0%	$ 104	$ 1,250	$ 1,558	-19.8%	
12	Totals			$ 1,496	$ 17,950	$ 18,258	-1.7%	
13			Number of Categories		9			
14			Average Spend	$ 1,994				
15			Min Spend	$ 1,200				
16			Max Spend					
17								

Budget Summary Budget Detail Mortgage Payments Car Lease Payments

Figure 14 MIN Function Added to the Budget Detail Worksheet

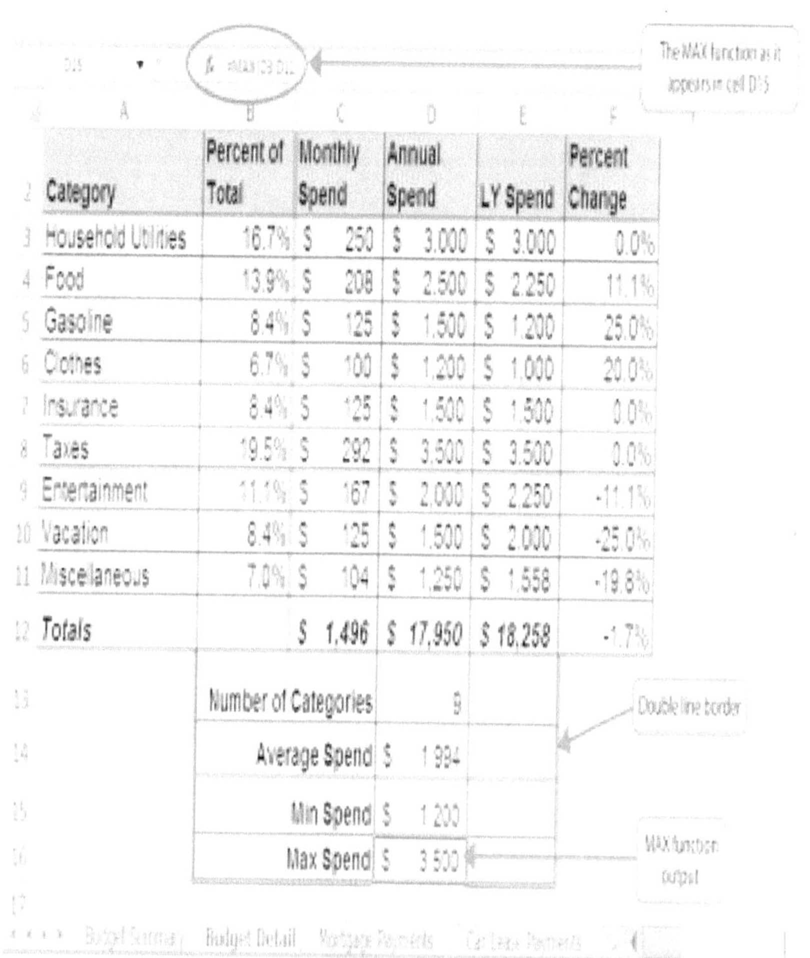

Figure 15 MAX Function Added to the Budget Detail Worksheet

Ability Refresher
Measurable Functions

Type an equivalent sign =.

Type the capacity name followed by an open bracket (or double-tap the capacity name from the capacity list.

Feature a range on a worksheet or snap singular cell areas followed by commas.

Type an end bracket) and press the ENTER key or press the ENTER key to close the capacity.

Reorder Formulas (Pasting without Formats)

Information record: Continue with CH2 Personal Budget.

As appeared in Figure 15, the COUNT, AVERAGE, MIN, and MAX capacities are summing up the information in the Annual Spend segment. You will likewise see that there is space to reorder these capacities under the LY Spend section. This permits us to analyze what we spent a year ago and what we intend to go through this year. Regularly, we would basically reorder these capacities into the range E13: E16. Nonetheless, you may have seen the twofold line style fringe that was utilized around the edge of the range B13: E16. In the event that we utilized the ordinary Paste order, the twofold line on the right side of the range would be supplanted with a solitary line. In this way, we are going to utilize one of the Paste Special orders to glue just the capacities with no of the organizing medicines. This is practiced through the accompanying advances:
Highlight range A2: F11 in the Detail worksheet.
Click Ribbon's Data tab.
Click the Sort&Filter command group button. This opens dialog Type, as shown in Figure 17.
Click the arrow to the "Sort by" box.
Click Total Percent from the drop-down list.
Click down arrow next to the Order sort box.
Click Largest to Smallest.
Click button Add Level. You can set a second level for any duplicate values in the Total Percent column.
Click the down arrow next to the "By" tab.
Select choice LY Invest. Leave the Sort Order to Largest
Click the OK button below the Sort dialog.
Save Personal Budget Ch2 tab.

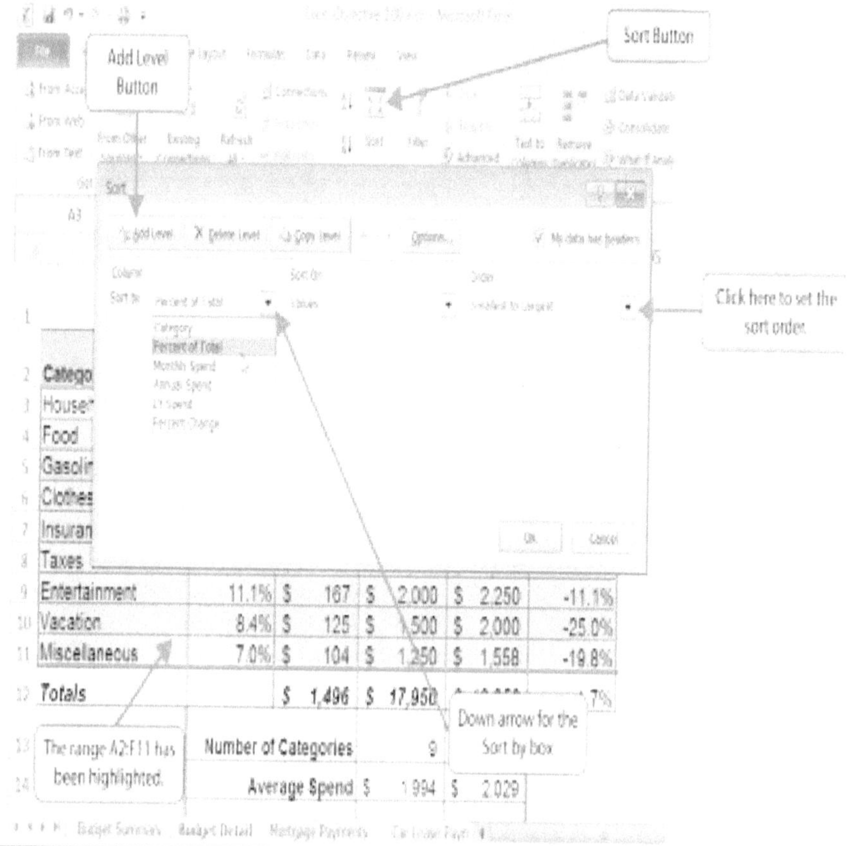

Figure 17 Sort box

Figure 18 shows the Budget Detail worksheet after sorting. Note that the Total Percent column has three identical values. For this worksheet, a second sort level had to be created. The second sort level arranges ascending values of 8.4 percent based on values in the LY Spend column. Excel provides you the choice to set as many sort levels as necessary for a worksheet.

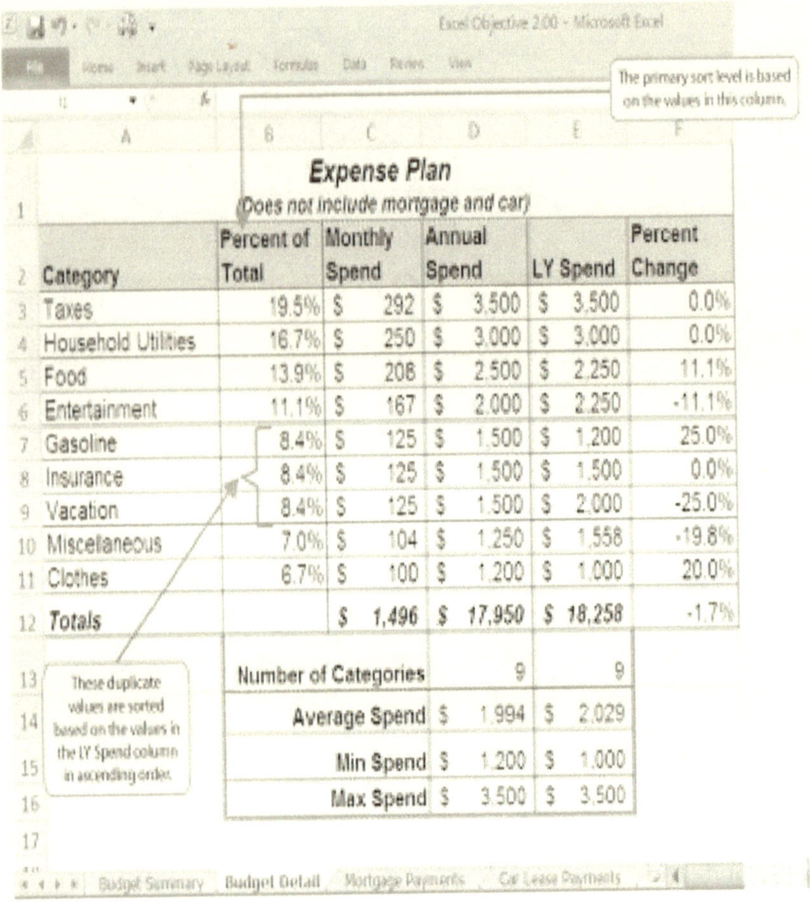

	A	B	C	D	E	F
1		**Expense Plan**				
		(Does not include mortgage and car)				
2	Category	Percent of Total	Monthly Spend	Annual Spend	LY Spend	Percent Change
3	Taxes	19.5%	$ 292	$ 3,500	$ 3,500	0.0%
4	Household Utilities	16.7%	$ 250	$ 3,000	$ 3,000	0.0%
5	Food	13.9%	$ 208	$ 2,500	$ 2,250	11.1%
6	Entertainment	11.1%	$ 167	$ 2,000	$ 2,250	-11.1%
7	Gasoline	8.4%	$ 125	$ 1,500	$ 1,200	25.0%
8	Insurance	8.4%	$ 125	$ 1,500	$ 1,500	0.0%
9	Vacation	8.4%	$ 125	$ 1,500	$ 2,000	-25.0%
10	Miscellaneous	7.0%	$ 104	$ 1,250	$ 1,558	-19.8%
11	Clothes	6.7%	$ 100	$ 1,200	$ 1,000	20.0%
12	Totals		$ 1,496	$ 17,950	$ 18,258	-1.7%
13		Number of Categories		9	9	
14		Average Spend		$ 1,994	$ 2,029	
15		Min Spend		$ 1,200	$ 1,000	
16		Max Spend		$ 3,500	$ 3,500	
17						

Figure 18 Budget Detail Worksheet

Refresher ability
Sorting (Multiple Levels)
Highlight a range of cells to sort.
Click Ribbon 's Data tab.
Click the Sort&Filter group button.
Select a "Sort by" drop-down column in the Sort dialog box.
Select a sort order from the drop-down list in the Sort dialog.
Click Add Level in the Sort dialog box.
Repeat steps 4-5.
Click the Sort dialog button, OK.
Now that the Budget Information worksheet is sorted, some key patterns can

easily be found. The exercise manual unmistakably shows that the best three classes as a level of complete going through for the year are charges, family unit utilities, and food. Each of the three classifications are necessities (or real factors) of life, and most family units normally require critical pay. Taking a gander at the Percent Change section, we can perceive how our arranged spending will change from a year ago. This is maybe the most significant worksheet segment since it permits you to evaluate whether your arrangement is practical. You'll see no planned changes for taxes and household utilities. While taxes can vary from year to year, predicting what they will be isn't too hard. In this situation, we believe that our budget does not affect tax costs. We also expect no improvement in household services. Such costs can also fluctuate annually. However, you can take steps to minimize costs, such as using less power, shutting off heat when nobody is in the room, keeping track of your wireless minutes, so you don't go past the limit allowed under your contract, etc. Accordingly, there is no change in arranged spending for family utilities as we will accept that any rate increments will be balanced with use decline. The third thing not to change is protection. Car and home insurance policies can adjust, but as with taxes, changes are predictable. Therefore, we assume no changes to our insurance policy.

The first big change in the worksheet is the Food and Entertainment divisions in rows 5 and 6. The Percent Change column reveals an 11.1% decline in entertainment consumption and an 11.1% rise in food spending. This is logical due to the fact that if you plan to eat less frequently in restaurants, you'll eat more often at home. While, in principle, this makes sense, it will be hard in reality. Dinners and fun groups can be hard to turn down. However, the entire process of keeping a budget is based on discipline, and it certainly takes a lot of discipline to plan and stick to targets for yourself.

Other points to note are changes in the gasoline and holiday categories. If you travel to school or work, gas prices can significantly impact your budget. If gas prices rise, it's important to be realistic, and you should reflect these increases in your budget. To compensate for increased gas spending, the vacation spending plan was reduced by 25%. Budgeting also involves some imagination. Although the holiday budget has been reduced, there is still money you can set aside to plan a spring break or winter break.

Finally, the budget shows a 19.8% reduction in Miscellaneous expenditures. This was defined as a group with multiple expenses like textbooks, school supplies, software updates, etc. (see Table 2.1). You can reduce spending in this category if you can use items like online textbooks. This spending reduction can free up funds for Clothes, a spending category that increased by 20%. We will further develop the Personal Budget Workbook in Section 2.3, "Personal Finance Functions."

Statistical functions are used when mathematical processes are required for a range of cells, such as summing values at multiple cell locations. For these calculations, functions are preferable to formulas, as adding many cell locations to a formula one at a time can be very time-consuming.
Statistical functions can be generated using comma-separated cell ranges or selected locations. Be sure that you use a cell range (two colon-separated cell locations) when applying a statistical function to a contiguous cell range.
To prevent Excel from modifying cell references in a formula or function when pasted to a new cell position, using a total reference. You could do this by placing a dollar sign) ($before a cell reference column and row number.
The # DIV/0 error appears when creating a formula that attempts to divide a constant or value by zero in a cell reference.
The Paste Formulas option is used to paste formulas without formatting treatments into cell locations that have already been formatted.

- You must set multiple levels or columns in the Sort dialog when sorting data containing multiple duplicate values.

USING SOLVER TO KNOW THE OPTIMAL PRODUCT MIX

This unit talks about utilizing Solver; a Microsoft Excel includes a program you can use to consider the possibility that examination, to decide an ideal item blend.

How might I decide the month to month item blend that expands benefit?

Organizations frequently need to decide the amount of every item to create on a month to month premise. In its least difficult structure, the item blend issue includes how to decide the measure of every item that ought to be created during a month to amplify benefits. Item blend should, for the most part, stick to the accompanying requirements:

· Product blend can't utilize a larger number of assets that are accessible.

· There is a constrained interest for every item. We can't create all the more an item during a month than request directs, in light of the fact that the overabundance creation is squandered (for instance, a transient medication).

We should now comprehend the accompanying case of the item blend issue. You can discover the answer to this issue in the record Prodmix.xlsx, which appeared in the Figure.

	B	C	D	E	F	G	H	I
2		Pounds made	150	160	170	180	190	200
3	Available	Product	1	2	3	4	5	6
4	4500	Labor	6	5	4	3	2.5	1.5
5	1600	Raw Material	3.2	2.6	1.5	0.8	0.7	0.3
6		Unit price	$ 12.50	$ 11.00	$ 9.00	$ 7.00	$ 6.00	$ 3.00
7		Variable cost	$ 6.50	$ 5.70	$ 3.60	$ 2.80	$ 2.20	$ 1.20
8		Demand	960	928	1041	977	1084	1055
9		Unit profit cont.	$ 6.00	$ 5.30	$ 5.40	$ 4.20	$ 3.80	$ 1.00
10								
11								
12		Profit	$ 4.504.00					
13					Available			
14		Labor Used	3695 <=		4500			
15		Raw Material Used	1488 <=		1600			

Suppose we work for a medication organization that produces six distinct items at their plant. The creation of every item requires work and crude material. Line 4 in the figure shows the long periods of work expected to deliver a pound of every item, and line 5 shows the pounds of crude material expected to create a pound of every item. For instance, delivering a pound of Product 1 requires six hours of work and 3.2 pounds of crude material. For each medication, the cost per pound is given in column 6, the unit cost per pound is given in line 7, and the benefit commitment per pound is given in line 9. For instance, Product 2 sells for $11.00 per pound, brings about a unit cost of $5.70 per pound, and contributes $5.30 benefit per pound. The month's interest for each medication is given in column 8. For instance, interest for Product 3 is 1041 pounds. This month, 4500 hours of work and 1600 pounds of crude material are accessible. By what method would this be able to organization amplify its month to month benefit?

On the off chance that we knew nothing about Excel Solver, we would tackle this issue by building a worksheet to follow benefit and asset use related to the item blend. At that point, we would utilize experimentation to fluctuate the item blend to streamline benefit without utilizing more work or crude material than is accessible, and without creating any medication in an overabundance of interest. We use Solver in this procedure just at the experimentation stage. Basically, Solver is an improved motor that impeccably plays out the experimentation search.

A vital aspect for taking care of the item blend issue is to proficiently figure the asset utilization and benefit related to some random item blend. A significant device that we can use to make this calculation is the SUMPRODUCT work. The SUMPRODUCT work increases relating values in cell ranges and return the whole of those qualities. Every cell extends utilized in a SUMPRODUCT assessment must have similar measurements, which infers that you can utilize SUMPRODUCT with two lines or two segments, yet not with one segment and one line.

For instance of how we can utilize the SUMPRODUCT work in our item blend model, we should attempt to figure our asset utilization. Our work use is determined by

(Work utilized per pound of medication 1)*(Drug 1 pounds produced)+

(Work utilized per pound of medication 2)*(Drug 2 pounds delivered) + ...

(Work utilized per pound of medication 6)*(Drug 6 pounds delivered)

We could figure work utilization in a progressively dull manner as D2*D4+E2*E4+F2*F4+G2*G4+H2*H4+I2*I4. So also, crude material utilization could be figured as D2*D5+E2*E5+F2*F5+G2*G5+H2*H5+I2*I5. Nonetheless, entering these recipes in a worksheet for six items is tedious. Envision to what extent it'd take if you were working with an organization that delivered, for instance, 50 items at their plant. A lot simpler approaches to figure work and crude material use are to duplicate from D14 to D15 the equation SUMPRODUCT($D$2:$I$2, D4:I4). This recipe processes D2*D4+E2*E4+F2*F4+G2*G4+H2*H4+I2*I4 (which is our work utilization) however is a lot simpler to enter! Notice that I utilize the $ sign with the range D2:I2, so when I duplicate the recipe, I, despite everything, catch the item blend from column 2. The equation in cell D15 registers crude material use.

Likewise, our benefit is controlled by

(Medication 1 benefit for each pound)*(Drug 1 pounds delivered) +

(Medication 2 benefit for each pound)*(Drug 2 pounds created) + ...

(Medication 6 benefit for each pound)*(Drug 6 pounds delivered)

The benefit is effortlessly figured in cell D12 with the recipe SUMPRODUCT(D9:I9,$D$2:$I$2).

We currently can recognize the three segments of our item blend Solver model.

· Target cell. We will likely augment benefits (registered in cell D12).

· Changing cells. The number of pounds created of every item (recorded in the cell extend D2:I2)

· Constraints. We have the accompanying limitations:
o Using no more labor or raw material than is available. That is, values in cells D14: D15 (resources used) must be less than or equal to values in cells

F14: F15 (resources available).

O Do not generate more drugs than is needed. That is, cell values D2: I2 (pounds produced from each drug) must be less than or equal to the demand for each drug (listed in cells D8: I8).

O We can't produce any drug negative.

I will show you the way to enter the target cell, change cells, and Solver constraints. Then click the Solve button to find a profit-maximizing product mix!

Click the Data tab to start and click Solver in the Analysis group.

Note: As described," Solver is activated by clicking the Microsoft Office button, followed by Add-Ins. Select Excel Add-ins in the Manage folder, check the Solver Add-in tab, then OK.

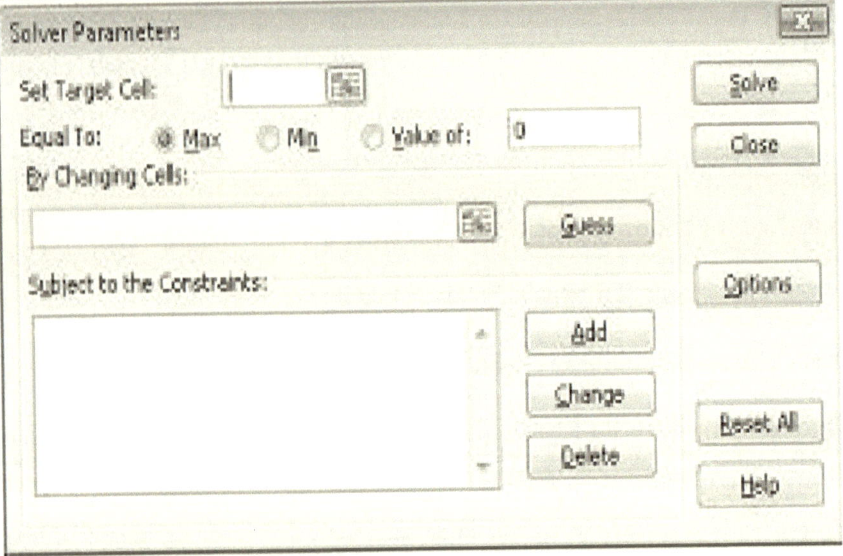

Click the Target Cell box, then select our profit cell (cell D12). Click the box By Changing Cells and point to range D2: I2, containing the pounds created by each drug.

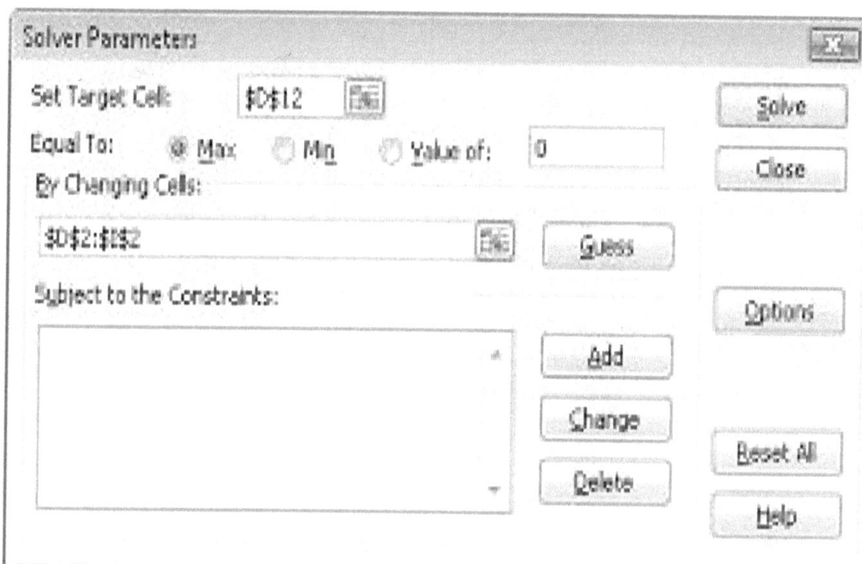

We are now able to add constraints. Click button Add. The Add Constraint discourse box appeared.

To include resource limitations, click the Cell Reference box and then pick D14:D15. Select < = from mid-list. Click the Constraint box and then select F14: F15.

We've now made sure that when Solver tries different values for changing cells, only combinations that satisfy both D14<=F14 (labor used is less than or equal to available labor) and D15<=F15 (the raw material used is less than or equal to available raw material) will be considered. Click Add to enter requirements.

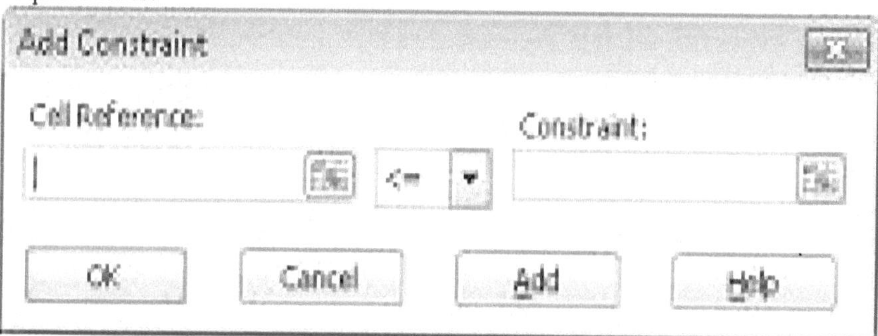

Adding these constraints ensures that only combinations satisfying the following parameters are considered when Solver tries different combinations for changing cell values:

· D2<=D8 (Drug 1 produced is less than or equal to Drug 1 demand)
· E2<=E8 (Drug 2 production is less than or equal to Drug 2 demand)
· F2<=F8 (Drug 3 produced is less than or equal to Drug 3 demand)
· G2<=G8 (Drug 4 produced is less than or equal to Drug 4 demand)
· H2<=H8 (Drug 5 produced is less than or equal to Drug 5 demand)
· I2<=I8 (Drug 6 produced is less than or equal to Drug 6 demand)

Click OK in the Constraint dialog box.

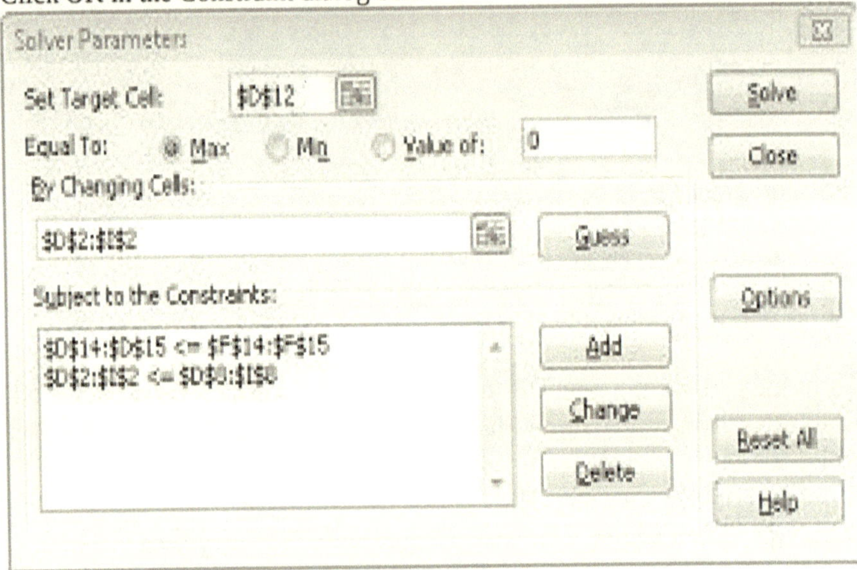

We enter the constraint that in the Solver Options dialog box, changing cells must be non-negative. Click the Solution Parameters dialog button. Check the Assume Linear Model box and Non-Negative box, as shown on the next page. Click Okay.

Solver Options

Max Time:	100	seconds	OK
Iterations:	100		Cancel
Precision:	0.000001		Load Model...
Tolerance:	5	%	Save Model...
Convergence:	0.0001		Help

☑ Assume Linear Model   ☐ Use Automatic Scaling
☑ Assume Non-Negative   ☐ Show Iteration Results

Estimates   Derivatives   Search
◉ Tangent   ◉ Forward   ◉ Newton
◯ Quadratic   ◯ Central   ◯ Conjugate

Checking the Assume Non-Negative box ensures Solver only considers combinations of changing cells where each changing cell accepts a non-negative worth. We checked the Assume Linear Model box in light of the fact that the issue of item blend is an exceptional Solver issue called a straight model.. A Solver model is basically linear under the following conditions:

· Target cell is determined by adding shape terms (changing cell)*(constant).

· Each constraint meets the 'linear model criterion,' meaning that each constraint is evaluated by adding the terms of the form (changing cell)*(constant) and comparing the quantities to a constant.

Why is the Solver problem linear? Our target cell (profit) is calculated

(Drug 1 profit per pound)*(Drug 1 pound)+

(Drug 2 profit per pound)*(Drug 2 pounds)+ ...

(Drug 6 / pound profit)*(Drug 6 pounds produced)

This estimation follows an example where the objective cell esteem is inferred by including structure terms (evolving cell)*(constant).

Our work limitation is assessed by looking at the worth got from (Labor utilized per pound of Drug 1)*(Drug 1 pound created)) + (Labor used per pound of Drug 2)*(Drug 2 pounds produced)+ ... (Labor used per pound of Drug 6)*(Drug 6 pounds produced) with the labor available.

Therefore, labor constraint is evaluated by combining the terms of the form (changing cell)*(constant) and comparing the sums to a constant. Labor constraints and raw material constraints meet linear model requirements.
Our requirements take shape
(Drug 1)<=(Drug 1 Demand)
(Produced)<=(Drug 2 Demand)
§
(Produced)<=(Drug 6 Demand)
Each demand constraint also meets the linear model requirement, as each is evaluated by adding the form terms (changing cell)*(constant) and comparing the sums to a constant.
Since our product mix model is a linear model, why would we care?
· If the Solver model is linear, and we pick Assume Linear Model, Solver guarantees the optimal solution for the Solver model. If a Solver model isn't straight, Solver may find the optimal solution.
· If the Solver model is linear, and we choose Assume Linear Model, Solver uses a very efficient algorithm (simplex method) to find the optimal solution. If the Solver model is straight and we don't select Assume Linear Model, Solver uses a very inefficient algorithm (the GRG2 method) and will have trouble finding the optimal solution for the model.

After clicking OK in the Solver Options window, we return to the key Solver dialog box shown in earlier. Clicking Solve computes an ideal arrangement (in the event that one exists) for our item blend model. An ideal answer for the item blend model would be a lot of changing cell esteems (pounds of each medication created) that augments benefit by and large achievable arrangements. Once more, a possible arrangement is a lot of changing cell esteems for all requirements. The increasing cell values shown are a feasible solution because all levels of production are non-negative, output levels do not exceed demand, and resource usage does not exceed available resources.

	Pounds made	150	160	170	180	190	200
Available Product		1	2	3	4	5	6
4500 Labor		6	5	4	3	2.5	1.5
1600 Raw Material		3.2	2.6	1.5	0.8	0.7	0.3
	Unit price	$ 12.50	$ 11.00	$ 9.00	$ 7.00	$ 6.00	$ 3.00
	Variable cost	$ 6.50	$ 5.70	$ 3.60	$ 2.80	$ 2.20	$ 1.20
	Demand	960	928	1041	977	1084	1055
	Unit profit cont.	$ 6.00	$ 5.30	$ 5.40	$ 4.20	$ 3.80	$ 1.80
	Profit	$ 4,504.00					
				Available			
	Labor Used	3695 <=		4500			
	Raw Material Used	1488 <=		1600			

For the following reasons, the cell changes shown on the next page reflect an infeasible solution:

· We generate more than Drug 5 requests.
· We use more labor than available.
· We use more raw material than available.

	Pounds made	300	0	0	0	1085	1000
Available Product		1	2	3	4	5	6
4500 Labor		6	5	4	3	2.5	1.5
1600 Raw Material		3.2	2.6	1.5	0.8	0.7	0.3
	Unit price	$ 12.50	$ 11.00	$ 9.00	$ 7.00	$ 6.00	$ 3.00
	Variable cost	$ 6.50	$ 5.70	$ 3.60	$ 2.90	$ 2.20	$ 1.20
	Demand	960	920	1041	977	1084	1055
	Unit profit cont.	$ 6.00	$ 5.30	$ 5.40	$ 4.20	$ 3.80	$ 1.00
	Profit	$ 7,723.00					
				Available			
	Labor Used	6012.5 <=		4500			
	Raw Material Used	2019.5 <=		1600			

Solver seeks the optimal solution after pressing Solve. To safeguard the ideal arrangement esteems in the worksheet, select Keep Solver Solution.

Our drug company could increase its monthly profit by producing 596.67 pounds of Drug 4, 1084 pounds of Drug 5, and none of the other drugs! We can't determine if we can otherwise achieve the $6,625.20 maximum profit. All we can be sure of is there's no way to make more than $6,627.20 this month with our limited resources and demand.

Does a Solver model have a solution at all times?

Assume that interest for every item should be met. We, at that point, need to change our interest limitations from D2:I2<=D8:I8 to D2:I2>=D8:I8. To have this done, open Solver, pick the D2:I2<=D8:I8 requirement, and afterward click Change. The Change Constraint discourse box, appeared, shows up.

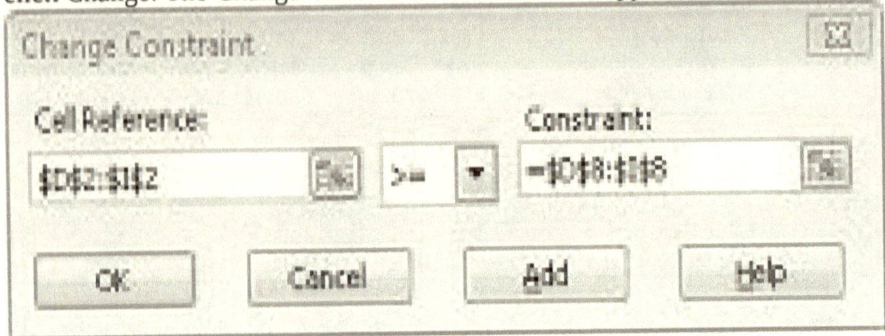

Select >=, and afterward click OK. We've currently guaranteed that Solver will consider changing just cell esteems that fulfill all needs. At the point when you click Solve, you'll see the message "Solver couldn't locate a plausible arrangement." This message doesn't imply that we committed an error in our model, yet rather that with our restricted assets, we can't satisfy the need for all items. The solver is basically disclosing to us that on the off chance that we need to fulfill the need for every item, we have to include more work, progressively crude materials, or a greater amount of both.

What does it mean when a Solver model yields the outcome Set Values Do Not Converge?

How about we see what occurs on the off chance that we permit boundless interest for every item, and we permit negative amounts to be delivered of each medication. (You can see this Solver issue on the Set Values Do Not Converge worksheet in the document Prodmix.xlsx.) To locate the ideal answer for this circumstance, open Solver, click the Options catch and clear the Assume Non-Negative box. In the Solver Parameters exchange box, select the interest requirement D2:I2<=D8:I8 and afterward click Delete to expel the imperative. At the point when you click Solve, Solver restores the message "Set Cell Values Do Not Converge." This message implies that if the objective cell is to be augmented (as in our model), there are achievable arrangements with self-assertively enormous objective cell esteems. (In the event that the objective cell is to be limited, the message "Set Cell Values Do

Not Converge" signifies there are doable arrangements with self-assertively little objective cell esteems.) In our circumstance, by permitting negative creation of a medication, we essentially "make" assets that can be utilized to deliver discretionarily a lot of different medications. Given our boundless interest, this permits us to make boundless benefits. In a genuine circumstance, we can't make an unending measure of cash. So, If by any chance, you see "Set Values Do Not Converge," your model has a blunder.

Issues

1. Assume our medication organization can buy as long as 500 hours of work at $1 more every hour than current work costs. How might we expand benefits?

2. At a chip fabricating plant, four professionals (A, B, C, and D) produce three items (Products 1, 2, and 3). This month, the chip producer can sell 80 units of Product 1, 50 units of Product 2, and at most 50 units of Product 3. Expert A can make just Products 1 and 3. Specialist B can make just Products 1 and 2. Expert C can make just Product 3. Expert D can make just Product 2. For every unit delivered, the items contribute the accompanying benefit: Product 1, $6; Product 2, $7; and Product 3, $10. The time (in hours) every professional need to make an item

4. Every professional can work as long as 120 hours of the month. In what capacity can the chip producer boost its month to month benefit? Accept a partial number of units can be created.

5. A PC fabricating plant produces mice, consoles, and computer game joysticks. The per-unit benefit, per-unit work utilization, month to month request, and per-unit machine-time use are given

6. Every month, a sum of 13,000 work hours and 3000 hours of machine time is accessible. By what means can the maker expand its month to month benefit commitment from the plant?

7. Resolve our medication model, expecting that a base interest of 200 units for each medication must be met.

8. Jason makes precious stone wristbands, pieces of jewelry, and studs. He

needs to work a limit of 160 hours out of each month. He has 800 ounces of precious stones. The benefit, work time, and ounces of precious stones required to deliver every item are given underneath. In the event that interest for every item is boundless, in what manner would Jason be able to expand his benefit?

SECURE YOUR WORKBOOK DATA AND DESIGN WITH A PASSWORD.

Step by step instructions to Protect Cells, Sheets, and Workbooks in Excel

At the point when it comes time to send your Excel spreadsheet, it's imperative to ensure the information that you're sharing. You should share your information; however, that doesn't mean it ought to be changed by another person.

Spreadsheets frequently contain basic information that shouldn't be adjusted or evacuated by the beneficiary. Fortunately, Excel has worked in highlights to ensure your spreadsheets.

In this instructional exercise, I'll assist you with ensuring that your Excel exercise manuals keep up information uprightness. Here are three key strategies you'll learn in this instructional exercise:

Secret word shield whole exercise manuals to keep them from being opened by unapproved clients.

Secure individual sheets and the exercise manual structure, to forestall the inclusion or erasure of sheets in the exercise manual.

Secure cells, to explicitly permit or deny changes to enter cells or equations in your Excel spreadsheets.

Indeed, even clients with the best expectations may coincidentally break a significant or complex equation. The best activity is to evacuate the alternative to change your spreadsheets through and through.

The most effective method to Protect Excel: Cells, Sheets, and Workbooks (Watch and Learn)

In the screencast underneath, you'll see my work through a few significant kinds of insurance in Excel. We'll secure a whole exercise manual, a solitary spreadsheet, and the sky is the limit from there.

Need a bit by bit walkthrough? Look at my means underneath to discover how to utilize these strategies. You'll figure out how to ensure your exercise manual in Excel, just as securing singular worksheets, cells, and how to work with cutting edge settings.

We start with more extensive worksheet insurances; at that point, work down to smaller focused on securities you can apply in Excel. How about we begin figuring out how to ensure your spreadsheet information:

Secret key Protect an Excel Workbook File.

How about we start off by securing a whole Excel record (or exercise manual) with a secret key to keep others from opening it.

This is a breeze to do. While working in Excel, explore to the File tab, pick the Info tab. Snap-on the Protect Workbook drop-down choice and pick Encrypt with Password.

Just like the case with any secret word, pick a solid and secure mix of letters, numbers, and characters, remembering that passwords are case-touchy.

Peruse to the File > Info tab, and pick Protect Workbook > Encrypt with the secret word.

It's critical to take note of that Microsoft has truly reinforced the reality of their secret key security in Excel. In earlier forms, there were simple workarounds to sidestep secret phrase security of Excel exercise manuals, yet not in more up to date forms.

Set an intricate secret key for the wellbeing of security, yet make a point to store it securely.

In Excel 2013 and past, secret word usage will forestall these conventional strategies to sidestep it. Ensure that you store your passwords cautiously and securely or you chance for all time losing access to your vital exercise manuals.

Excel Workbook - Mark as Final

In a situation where you've to be somewhat less compelling with your spreadsheets, think about utilizing the Mark as Final element. At the point when you mark an Excel document as the last form, it changes the record to peruse just mode, and the client should re-empower altering.

To change a document to peruse just mode, come back to the File > Info catch and snap-on Protect Workbook once more. Snap-on Mark as Final and affirm that you need to stamp the archive as the last form.

Imprint a record as the last form to leave a delicate admonition for clients of that document.

Denoting a record as the last form will add a delicate admonition to the highest point of the document. Any individual who opens the document after it has been set apart as definite will see a notification, cautioning them that the record is finished.

At the point when a document is set apart as the last form, the exercise manual will show this.

Denoting a document as the last form is a less conventional method of flagging that a record shouldn't be changed further. The beneficiary, despite everything, can click Edit Anyway and adjust the spreadsheet. Denoting a document as the last version is increasingly similar to a recommendation; however, it's an extraordinary methodology on the off chance that you confide in the other record clients.

Secret phrase Protect Your Excel Sheet Structure.

Next up, how about we figure out how to secure the structure of an Excel exercise manual. This choice will guarantee that no sheets are erased, included, or re-masterminded within the exercise manual.

In a situation where you need everybody to have the option to get to the exercise manual, however, limit the progressions they can make to a record; this is an incredible beginning. This secures the structure of the exercise manual and cutoff points on how the client can wash the bed covers within it.

To turn on this assurance, go to the Review tab on Excel's strip and snap-on Protect Workbook.

Discover the Review tab, click on Protect Workbook, and set a secret word to secure the structure of your Excel exercise manual.

When this alternative is turned on, the accompanying will become effective:

No new sheets could be included to the exercise manual.

No sheets can be erased from the exercise manual.

Sheets can never again be concealed or unhidden from the client's view.

The client can not drag anymore and drop the sheet tabs to reorder them in the exercise manual.

Obviously, I believed clients could be given the secret word to unprotect the exercise manual and adjust it. To unprotect an exercise manual, essentially click on the Protect Workbook button again and input the secret phrase to unprotect the Excel exercise manual.

Snap Protect Workbook a subsequent time and information the secret key to re-empower exercise manual changes.

The most effective method to Protect Cells in Excel

Presently, how about we get down to truly definite strategies for securing a spreadsheet. Up until this point, we've been a secret phrase securing a whole exercise manual or the structure of an Excel document. In this segment, we dive into how to secure your cells in Excel with explicit settings you can apply. We spread how to permit or square specific kinds of changes to be made to parts of your spreadsheet.

To begin, discover Excel's Review tab, and snap-on Protect Sheet. On the spring up window, you'll see a tremendous arrangement of alternatives. This window permits you to adjust how you need to secure the cells in your Excel spreadsheet. For the present, we should leave the settings at their default.

To ensure a sheet, select a tab in your Excel exercise manual, click on the Review tab and pick the Protect Sheet menu alternative.

This choice takes into consideration quite certain assurances of your spreadsheet. As a matter of course, the choices will thoroughly secure the spreadsheet. We should include a secret word with the goal that the sheet is secured. In the event that you press OK now, how about we see what happens when you endeavor to change a cell.

After a sheet has been secured, endeavoring to change a phone will yield this blunder message.

Exceed expectations lose a mistake that the cell is ensured, which is actually what we needed.

Fundamentally, this alternative is pivotal on the off chance that you need to guarantee that your spreadsheet isn't changed by other people who approach the document. Utilizing the secure sheet include is a way that you can specifically ensure the spreadsheet.

To unprotect the sheet, basically, click on the Protect Sheet catch and reappear the secret word to expel the securities added to the sheet.

Explicit Protections in Excel

How about we investigate the choices that show when you begin to secure a sheet in Excel exercise manuals.

Secret word secure worksheet cells in Excel choices.

The Protect Sheet menu allows you to refine the alternatives for sheet security. Each of the cases on this menu lets the client change marginally increasingly within an ensured worksheet.

To expel insurance, check the separate box in the rundown. For instance, you could permit the spreadsheet client to Format cells by checking the comparing box.

Here are two thoughts on how you could specifically permit the client to change the spreadsheet:

Check the Format cells, segments, and columns boxes to let the client change the visual appearance of cells without adjusting the first information.

Supplement sections and columns could be checked with the goal that the client can include more information while ensuring the first cells.

The significant box to leave checked is the Protect worksheet and substance of bolted cells box. This secures the information within cells.

At the point when you're working with essential budgetary information or recipes that will be utilized in deciding, you need to keep up control of the information and guarantee that it doesn't change. Utilizing these kinds of focused insurances is a significant Excel ability to ace.

Recap and Keep Learning More About Excel

Bolting up a spreadsheet before you send it is urgent to ensuring your significant information and ensuring that it's not abused. The tips I partook in this instructional exercise assist you with keeping up control of that information much after your Excel spreadsheet is sent and shared.

These tips are extra instruments and steps to turning into a progressed Excel client. Ensuring your exercise manuals is a particular aptitude, yet there are bunches of approaches to improve your presentation. As usual, there's space to become your Excel abilities further. Here are some useful Excel instructional exercises with significant aptitudes to ace straightaway:

PivotTables are an extraordinary device for working with spreadsheet information. Here are 5 Advanced Excel Pivot Table Techniques you can adapt now.

ExcelZoo has a posting of extra instructional exercises for ensuring your exercise manuals, sheets, and cells.

- Condition designing changes how a cell looks dependent on what's within it.

IMPROVE BUSINESS ANALYSES BY ADDING INTELLIGENCE AND KNOWLEDGE TO YOUR MODELS

The Importance of Excel in Business
Microsoft (NASDAQ: MSFT) Excel was discharged in 1985 and has developed to turn out to be apparently the most significant PC program in work environments around the globe. , you, by and large, would utilize Excel. In business, truly, any capacity in any industry can profit by those with solid Excel information. Exceed expectations are an integral asset that has gotten settled in business forms around the world - regardless of whether for breaking down stocks or guarantors, planning, or sorting out customer deals records.

Money and Accounting

Monetary administrations and budgetary bookkeeping are the territories of funds that depend on and advantage from Excel spreadsheets the most. During the 1970s and mid-1980s, monetary experts would go through weeks running propelled recipes either physically or in programs like IBM's (NYSE: IBM) Lotus 1-2-3. Presently, you can perform complex displays in minutes with Excel.

Stroll through the fund or bookkeeping branch of any major corporate office, and you will see PC screens loaded up with Excel spreadsheets doing the math, illustrating monetary outcomes, and making financial plans, estimates, and plans used to settle on significant business choices.

START

Most clients realize that Excel can include, take away, increase, and separation, however, it can do significantly more with cutting edge IF capacities when combined with VLOOKUP, INDEX-MATCH-MATCH, and turntables. (For additional, see the Investopedia Guide To Excel For Finance: PV And FV Functions.)

Showcasing and Product Management

While showcasing and item experts look to their fund groups to do the truly difficult work for budgetary examination, utilizing spreadsheets to list client and deals targets can assist you with dealing with your salesforce and plan future advertising techniques dependent on past outcomes.

Utilizing a turntable, clients can rapidly and effectively sum up clients and deals information by class with a brisk intuitive.

HR Planning

While database frameworks like Oracle (ORCL), (SAP), and Quickbooks (INTU) can be utilized to oversee finance and representative data, sending out that information into Excel permits clients to find patterns, sum up costs and hours by payroll interval, month, or year, and better see how your workforce is spread out by capacity or pay level.

HR experts can utilize Excel to take a goliath spreadsheet loaded with representative information and see precisely where the expenses are coming from and how to best arrangement and control them for what's to come.

You Can Do Anything With a Spreadsheet

Utilizing Excel for business has basically no restrictions for applications. Here are a few models:

When arranging a group excursion to a ball game, you can utilize Excel to follow the RSVP rundown and expenses.

Exceed expectations make income development models for new items dependent on new client conjectures.

When arranging an article schedule for a site, you can drill down dates and points in a spreadsheet.

While making a financial plan for a little item, you can list cost classes in a spreadsheet, update it month to month and make a graph to show how close the item is to spending plan over every classification.

You can compute client limits dependent on month to month buy volume by item.

Clients can sum up client income by item to discover regions where to assemble a more grounded client connections.

Utilize complex computation techniques, as Sharpe proportions.

Exceed expectations isn't going anyplace

Exceed expectations aren't going anyplace, and organizations will keep on utilizing Excel as an essential instrument for different capacities and applications running from IT anticipates to organization picnics.

A piece of working information on Excel is essential for most office-based experts today, and more grounded Excel aptitudes can make way for advancement and administration openings. Exceed expectations are an amazing asset yet can't work alone. It takes a smart PC client to exploit everything Excel brings to the table to give the best outcomes to their organization.

CALCULATE LOAN PAYMENTS, INTEREST COSTS, TERMS, AND AMORTIZATION SCHEDULES

Credit reimbursement is the demonstration of taking care of cash recently obtained from a loan specialist, ordinarily through a progression of occasional installments that incorporate head in addition to premium. Did you realize you can utilize the product program Excel to ascertain your credit reimbursements?

Key Takeaways

Use Excel to understand your home loan through deciding your regularly scheduled installment, your financing cost, and your credit plan.
You can take a more top to bottom glance at the breakdown of an advance with exceed expectations and make a reimbursement plan that works for you. There are counts accessible for each progression that you can change to meet your particular needs.

Separating and looking at your credit bit by bit can cause the reimbursement procedure to feel not so much overpowering but rather more reasonable.

Understanding Your Mortgage

Utilizing Excel, you can show signs of improvement comprehension of your home loan in three straightforward advances. The initial step decides the regularly scheduled installment. The subsequent advance figures the financing cost, and the third step decides the advance timetable.

You can manufacture a table in Excel that will disclose to you the financing cost, the credit estimation for the span of the advance, the disintegration of the advance, the amortization, and the regularly scheduled installment.

Figure the Monthly Payment

In the first place, here are the means by which to compute the regularly scheduled installment for a home loan. Utilizing the yearly loan cost, the head, and the length, we can decide the sum to be reimbursed month to month.

The recipe, as appeared in the screen capture above, is composed as follows:

=-PMT(rate;length;express value;[type])
The short sign before PMT is important as the equation restores a negative number. The initial three contentions are the pace of the credit, the length of the advance (number of periods), and the chief acquired. The last two contentions are discretionary; the remaining worth defaults to zero, payable ahead of time (for one) or toward the end (for zero), is likewise discretionary.

The Excel recipe used to figure the regularly scheduled installment of the advance is:

=-PMT((1+B2)^(1/12)-   1;B4*12;B3)   =   PMT((1+3,10%)^(1/12)-1;10*12;120000)

Clarification: For the rate, we utilize the month to month rate (time of rate), at that point, we ascertain the number of periods (120 for a long time duplicated by a year) and, at last, we show the chief acquired. Our regularly scheduled installment will be $1,161.88 for more than ten years.

Compute the Annual Interest Rate

We have perceived how to set up the estimation of a regularly scheduled installment for a home loan. Yet, we might need to set a greatest regularly scheduled installment that we can bear the cost of that likewise shows the number of years over which we would need to reimburse the advance. Therefore, we might want to realize the relating yearly financing cost.

As appeared in the screen capture above, we initially ascertain the period rate (month to month, for our situation), and afterward, the yearly rate. The equation utilized will be RATE, as appeared in the screen capture above. It is composed below:

=RATE(Nper;pmt;present_value;[future_value];[type])

The initial three contentions are the length of the credit (number of periods), the regularly scheduled installment to reimburse the advance, and the chief obtained. The last three contentions are discretionary, and the leftover worth defaults to zero; the term contention for dealing with the development ahead of time (for one) or toward the end (for zero) is likewise discretionary. At last, the gauge contention is discretionary yet can give an underlying assessment of the rate.

The Excel equation used to figure the loaning rate is:

=RATE(12*B4;- B2;B3) = RATE(12*13;- 960;120000)

Note: the relating information in the regularly scheduled installment must be offered a negative hint. This is the reason there's less sign before the recipe. The rate time frame is 0.294%.

We utilize the equation = (1 + B5) is 12-1 ^ = (1 + 0.294 %) ^ 12-1 to acquire the yearly pace of our advance, which is 3.58%. At the end of the day, to acquire $120,000 more than 13 years to pay $960 month to month, we ought to arrange credit at a yearly 3.58% greatest rate.

Utilizing Excel is an incredible method of monitoring what you owe and thinking of a timetable for reimbursement that limits any charges that you may wind up owing.
Determining the Length of a Loan
We will presently perceive how to decide the length of credit when you know the yearly rate, the chief acquired, and the regularly scheduled installment that will be reimbursed. As it were, to what extent will we have to reimburse a $120,000 contract with a pace of 3.10% and a regularly scheduled installment of $1,100?

The recipe we will utilize is NPER, as appeared in the screen capture above, and it is composed as follows:

=NPER(rate;pmt;present_value;[future_value];[type])

The initial three contentions are the yearly pace of the credit, the regularly scheduled installment expected to reimburse the advance, and the chief obtained. The last two contentions are discretionary, the leftover worth defaults to zero. The term contention payable ahead of time (for one) or toward the end (for zero) is additionally discretionary.

=NPER((1+B2)^(1/12)-   1;-   B4;B3)   =   NPER((1+3,10%)^(1/12)-   1;-1100;120000)

Note: the relating information in the regularly scheduled installment must be offered a negative hint. This is the reason we have less sign before the recipe. The repayment length is 127.97 periods (months for our situation).

We will utilize the equation = B5/12 = 127.97/12 for the number of years to finish the advance reimbursement. At the end of the day, to acquire $120,000, with a yearly pace of 3.10% and to pay $1,100 month to month, we ought to compensate developments for 128 months or ten years and eight months.

Breaking down the Loan
An advance installment is made out of head and intrigue. The intrigue is determined for every period—for instance, the month to month reimbursements more than ten years will give us 120 periods.

The contentions of the two recipes are the equivalent and are separated as follows:

=-PPMT(rate;num_period;length;principal;[residual];[term])

The contentions are equivalent to for the PMT equation previously observed, aside from "num_period," which is added to show the period over which to separate the advance given the head and intrigue. Here's a model:

=-PPMT((1+B2)^(1/12)-   1;1;B4*12;B3)   =   PPMT((1+3,10%)^(1/12)-1;1;10*12;120000)

The outcome is appeared in the screen capture above "Advance Decomposition" over the period examined, which is "one;" that is, the primary time frame or the principal month. We pay $1,161.88 separated into $856.20 head and $305.68 intrigue.

Advanced Computation in Excel

It is additionally conceivable to compute the head and intrigue reimbursement for a few periods, for example, the initial a year or the initial 15 months.

=-CUMPRINC(rate;length;principal;start_date;end_date;type)

We discover the contentions, rate, length, head, and term (which are required) that we previously found in the initial segment with the recipe PMT. In any case, here, we need the "start_date" and "end_date" contentions too. The "start_date" demonstrates the start of the period to be broken down, and the "end_date" shows the finish of the period to be dissected.

Here's a model:

=-CUMPRINC((1+B2)^(1/12)- 1;B4*12;B3;1;12;0)

The outcome is appeared in the screen capture "Cumul first year," so the broke down periods extend from one to 12 of the main time frame (first month) to the (twelfth month). Longer than a year, we would pay $10,419.55 in head and $ 3,522.99 in intrigue.

Amortization of the Loan
The earlier recipes permit us to make our calendar period by period, to realize the amount we will pay month to month in head and intrigue, and to realize what amount is left to pay.
Creating a Loan Schedule
To do this, we will utilize the various recipes talked about above and extend them over the number of periods.
In the principal time frame section, enter "1" as the main time frame and afterward drag the cell down. For our situation, we need 120 periods since a 10-year advance installment duplicated by a year approaches 120.

The subsequent section is the month to month sum we have to pay every month—which is steady over the whole advance calendar. To ascertain the sum, embed the accompanying equation inside the cell of the first period:

=-PMT(TP-1;B4*12;B3) =-PMT((1+3,10%)^(1/12)- 1;10*12;120000)

The third segment is the primary that will be reimbursed month to month. For instance, for the 40th period, we will reimburse $945.51 in head-on our month to month aggregate sum of $1,161.88.

To figure the chief sum recovered, we utilize the accompanying equation:

=-PPMT(TP;A18;$B$4*12;$B$3)   =-
PPMT((1+3,10%)^(1/12);1;10*12;120000)

The 4th section is the enthusiasm, for which we utilize the equation to figure the head reimbursed on our month to month add up to find how much intrigue is to be paid:

=-INTPER(TP;A18;$B$4*12;$B$3)   =-
INTPER((1+3,10%)^(1/12);1;10*12;120000)

The fifth segment contains the sum left to pay. For instance, after the 40th installment, we should pay $83,994.69 on $120,000.

The equation is as per the following:

=$B$3+CUMPRINC(TP;$B$4*12;$B$3;1;A18;0)

The equation utilizes a blend of the head under a period in front of the cell containing the chief acquired. This period starts to change when we duplicate and drag the cell down.

Credit Amortization with Microsoft Excel

Is it true that you are an understudy? Did you realize that Amazon is offering a half year of Amazon Prime - free two-day delivery, free motion pictures, and different advantages - to understudies?

Snap here to find out additional

This is the first of a two-section instructional exercise on amortization plans. In this instructional exercise, we will perceive how to make an amortization plan for a fixed-rate credit utilizing Microsoft Excel and different spreadsheets (the following part tells the best way to deal with additional chief installments and furthermore incorporates an example spreadsheet utilizing this equivalent model information). Practically the entirety of this instructional exercise likewise applies to for all intents and purposes all other spreadsheet projects, for example, Open Office Calc and Google Docs and Spreadsheets. Spreadsheets have numerous points of interest over money related number crunchers for this reason, including adaptability, convenience, and design capacities.

Completely amortizing advances are very normal. Models incorporate home loans, vehicle credits, and so on. Commonly, however, not generally, a completely amortizing credit is one that calls for equivalent installments (annuity) for the duration of the life of the advance. The advance parity is completely resigned after the last installment is made. Every installment in this kind of credit comprises of intrigue and head installments. It is the nearness of the vital installment that gradually diminishes the credit balance, inevitably to $0. On the off chance that additional chief installments are made, at that point, the rest of the equalization will decrease more rapidly than the credit contract initially envisioned.

An amortization plan is a table which presents each advance installment and a breakdown of the measure of intrigue and head. Commonly, it will likewise show the rest of the equalization after every installment has been made.

Figuring Interest and Principal in a Single Payment

We should begin by investigating the rudiments with a model credit (on the off chance that you definitely know the nuts and bolts, you can jump right to Creating an Amortization Schedule):

Envision that you are going to take out a 30-year fixed-rate contract. The particulars of the credit indicate an underlying chief parity (the sum acquired) of $200,000 and an APR of 6.75%. Installments will be made month to month. What will be the regularly scheduled installment? What amount of the primary installment will be intrigued, and what amount of will be head?

Our primary goal is to ascertain the regularly scheduled installment sum. We can do this most effectively by utilizing Excel's PMT work. Note that since we are making regularly scheduled installments, we should change the number of periods (NPer) and the loan fee (Rate) to month to month esteems. We will do this inside the PMT work itself. Open another spreadsheet and enter the information as demonstrated as follows:

	A	B	C	D	E	F
1	**Loan Data**					
2	Original Principal	$ 200,000				
3	Loan Term (Years)	30				
4	Annual Interest Rate	6.75%				
5	Payments per Year	12				
6	Payment	$ 1,297.20	←———— =PMT(B4/B5,B3*B5,-B2)			

Review that the PMT work is characterized as:

PMT(Rate,NPer,PV,FV,Type)

Where Rate is the per period loan cost and NPer is the all outnumber of periods. For this situation, as appeared in the image, we figure the Rate with B4/B5 (0.5625% every month), and NPer is B3*B5 (360 months). PV is entered as - B2 (- 200,000, negative since we need the response to be a positive number). You can see that the regularly scheduled installment is $1,297.20. (Note that your genuine home loan installment would be higher on the grounds that it would probably incorporate protection and property charge installments that would be channeled into an escrow account by the home loan administration organization.)

That addresses our first inquiry. Along these lines, we currently need to isolate that installment into its advantage and head segments. We can do this utilizing a few straightforward equations (we will utilize some inherent capacities in a second):

Month to month Interest Payment = Principal Balance x Monthly Interest Rate.

Month to month Principal Payment = Monthly Payment - Monthly Interest Payment

Utilizing these recipes, we can see that the intriguing part of the principal installment would be:

Enthusiasm for first Payment = 200,000 x 0.005625 = $1,125   also, the essential installment is:

Head in first Payment = 1,297.20 - 1,125 = $172.20

Note that the whole of the intrigue and chief is the measure of the complete installment:

1,125 + 172.20 = $1,297.20

That is the situation for each and every installment over the life of the advance. Be that as it may, as installments are made, the chief equalization will decrease. This, thus, implies the intrigue installment will be lower, and the central installment will be higher (in light of the fact that the absolute installment sum is consistent), for each progressive installment.

Utilizing the Built-in Functions
We've presently perceived how the head and intrigue parts of every installment are determined. Irrespectively, you could utilize two or three implicit capacities to crunch the numbers for you. These capacities likewise make it simpler to figure the head or potential enthusiasm for any discretionary installment.

The two capacities from the Finance menu that we are going to utilize are the IPMT (intrigue installment) and the PPMT (head installment) capacities. These capacities ascertain the measure of intrigue or chief paid for some random installment. They are characterized as:

IPMT(Rate, Per, NPer, PV, FV, Type)

PPMT(Rate, Per, NPer, PV, FV, Type)

Thus, utilizing our information from above, we can compute the measure of enthusiasm for the principal installment with:

=IPMT(B4/B5,1,B3*B5,- B2)

What's more, we get $1,125. The measure of the head in the primary installment is:

=PPMT(B4/B5,1,B3*B5,- B2)

Which gives $172.20. Those answers coordinate precisely the ones that we determined physically above. Note that in the two capacities, we determined that Per (the installment time frame) is 1 for the principal installment. We would indicate 2 for the subsequent installment, etc. Clearly, we will utilize a cell reference in our amortization table.

Exceed expectations doesn't have a worked incapacity to figure the rest of the equalization after an installment; however, we can do that effectively enough with a straightforward equation. Basically, take the starting equalization less the chief paid in the primary installment, and you will find that the rest of the parity after one installment is $199,827.80:

Chief Balance After first Payment = 200,000 - 172.20 = $199,827.80

Making an Amortization Schedule
As noted at the outset, an amortization plan is basically a posting of every installment and the breakdown of intrigue, head, and remaining parity. For this advance, an amortization table for the initial a half year would resemble this:

	A	B	C	D	E
1	**Loan Data**				
2	Original Principal	$ 200,000			
3	Loan Term (Years)	30			
4	Annual Interest Rate	6.75%			
5	Payments per Year	12			
6	Payment	$1,297.20			
7					
8	**Month**	**Payment**	**Interest**	**Principal**	**Balance**
9	0				200,000.00
10	1	1,297.20	1,125.00	172.20	199,827.80
11	2	1,297.20	1,124.03	173.16	199,654.64
12	3	1,297.20	1,123.06	174.14	199,480.50
13	4	1,297.20	1,122.08	175.12	199,305.38
14	5	1,297.20	1,121.09	176.10	199,129.28
15	6	1,297.20	1,120.10	177.09	198,952.18

The principal thing that we need to do is to set up the table beginning with the marks in A8:E8. Presently, in section A we need a progression of numbers from 0 to 360 (the most extreme number of installments that we will permit). To make this arrangement, select A9 and afterward pick Edit » Fill » Series from the menus. This will dispatch the Series discourse box. Fill it in precisely as appeared, and afterward click the Ok button.

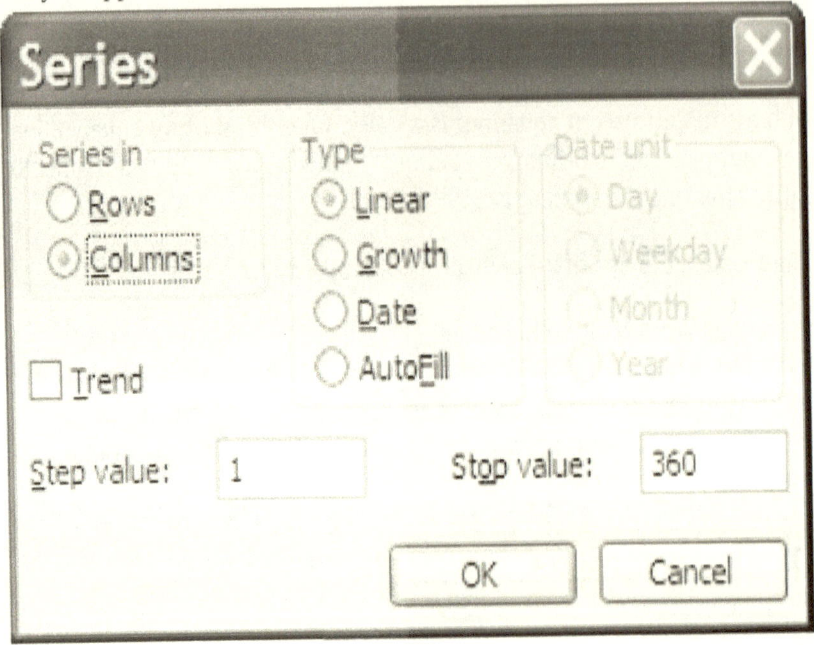

Now, we are prepared to fill in the equations. Start with the starting head in E9 with the equation: =B2. That will connect it to the chief parity as given in the info zone. Presently, select B10 and enter the recipe:

=PMT(B$4/B$5,B$3*B$5,- B$2)

Also, you will see that the regularly scheduled installment is $1,297.20, as appeared previously. In C10 we will figure the intriguing bit of the principal installment with the recipe:

=IPMT(B$4/B$5,A10,B$3*B$5,- B$2)

The chief segment of the installment can be determined, in D10 with:

=PPMT (B$4/B$5,A10,B$3*B$5,- B$2)

At last, we figure the rest of the offset in E10 with the equation:

=E9-D10

Check your outcomes against those appeared above, being mindful so as to type the recipes precisely as appeared (the $ are significant on the grounds that they freeze the cell references with the goal that they don't change when we duplicate the equations down). When your outcomes in column 10 match the image, duplicate the equations right down to the finish of the table in line 369. (Note: The most straightforward approach to do this is to choose B10:E10 and afterward double-tap the AutoFill handle in the lower right corner of the choice. This will duplicate the recipes as far as possible of the present range, which is characterized by the last information point in section A.)

You would now be able to go into the info territory (B2:B5) and change the advance terms. The amortization timetable will naturally recalculate.

Make the Amortization Schedule Fancy
For no particular reason and some usefulness, I liked it up a piece by utilizing a few IF articulations, restrictive organizing, and making a graph that shows the rest of the parity after some time. Despite the fact that these things are, for the most part, for looks, they additionally improve the usefulness of the spreadsheet. I'll experience every one of these individually.

Utilizing IF Statements in the Formulas
The recipes that we entered above for the installment, intrigue, head, and remaining equalization will work more often than not. Notwithstanding, they can offer out of control responses in specific situations. For instance, after the last installment is made, the rest of the parity might be shown as 0; however, Excel may believe that it is truly something like 0.0000000015. This is because of a few elements, including the way that PCs do math (in twofold rather than decimal, and the transformations aren't generally great). Along these lines, it is useful to change the aftereffects of our equations once the rest of the parity is sufficiently little to adequately be 0. On the off chance that the rest of the parity is sufficiently little, at that point, I'm going to advise the equations to regard it as 0. To do this, I'm utilizing the Round capacity to

adjust the rest of the equalization to 5 decimal spots to one side of the decimal point. The table beneath shows the recipes that you ought to go into B10:E10 and afterward duplicate down the as far as possible of the table.

Cell	Formula
B10	=IF(ROUND(E9,5)>0,B$6,0)
C10	=IF(B10>0,IPMT(B$4/B$5,A10,B$3*B$5,-B$2),0)
D10	=IF(B10>0,PPMT(B$4/B$5,A10,B$3*B$5,-B$2),0)
E10	=IF(ROUND(E9,5)>0,E9-D10,0)

Once more, the main change is that the recipes first verify whether the rest of the parity is basically zero in the event that not, at that point, they compute regularly. Assuming this is the case, at that point, they return 0.

Utilize Conditional Formatting to Make it Pretty

Review that we set up this spreadsheet so it could deal with a limit of 30 years of regularly scheduled installments. What might occur if the credit term was not as much as that (state, 15 years)? All things considered, you would wind up with a lot of lines with zeros in them after the advance is paid off. Terrible.

This could be fixed with the Conditional Formatting usefulness that is worked into ongoing variants of Excel. Essentially, we'd prefer to make those "vacant" cells vanish. On the off chance, that would likewise be pleasant on the off chance that we could underline the last installment also.

To start with, select cells A10:E369 since we will apply the designing to every one of them immediately. Presently, go to Format » Conditional Formatting from the menus. That will dispatch the accompanying discourse box.

Notice that I have set two contingent arrangements. The primary (Condition 1) is the most significant. It sets the content shading to white for any cells after the last installment has been made. This successfully shrouds them, yet the equations are still there. We can decide whether a phone is after the last installment by looking at the installment number (in section A) with the all outnumber of installments (B3*B5).

I am utilizing the "Recipe Is" choice, so select that starting from the drop rundown and afterward enter the equation: =$A10>($B$3*$B$5) and type it precisely. A relative reference is the $A10 so that in the accompanying segment, it will change to $A11, at that point $A12, etc. Presently, press the Format catch and set the text style shading to white.

The second restrictive organization basically underlines the absolute last installment. Along these lines, we get a visual sign that we have arrived at the finish of the table. For this situation, we are going to utilize nearly a similar rationale, then again, actually, we are trying to check whether we are at the last installment, instead of after it. Press the Add >> catch to include this condition. The equation is =$A10=($B$3*$B$5). Once more, type it precisely. Presently, press the Format button, and go to the Border tab and set an underline outskirt.

Press the OK catch to complete the organizing and come back to the spreadsheet. It should seem as though nothing has occurred. Presently, change the incentive in B3 (the number of years) to 15. Look down the worksheet, and you should see an underlined after installment 180 and that the entirety of the cells beneath that is clear. Cool, huh?

Make a Chart

The last improvement that I have made is to make an outline that shows the rest of the parity declining after some time. Essentially, you should simply choose A8:A369 and E8:E369 and afterward make an XY Scatter outline. I've liked it up a tad with a live diagram title and a parchment bar; however, I'll leave those highlights to another instructional exercise. The conclusive outcome is demonstrated as follows.

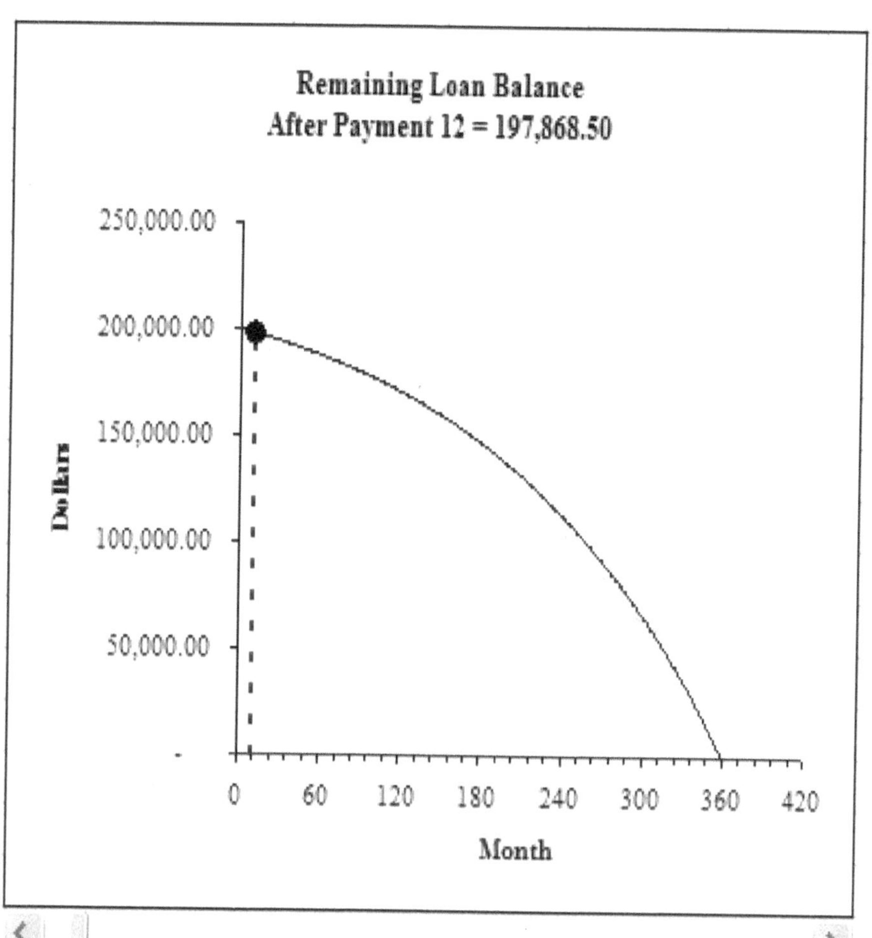

Remaining Loan Balance
After Payment 12 = 197,868.50
Dollars
Month
250,000.00
200,000.00
150,000.00
100,000.00
50,000.00
0
60
120
180
240
300
360
420